BREAK THE DEALER

Also by Jerry L. Patterson

BLACKJACK: A WINNER'S HANDBOOK

BLACKJACK'S WINNING FORMULA

CASINO GAMBLING

SPORTS BETTING

BREAK THE DEALER

Winning Strategies for *Today's* Blackjack

Jerry L. Patterson and Eddie Olsen

A Perigee Book

Perigee Books
are published by
The Putnam Publishing Group
200 Madison Avenue
New York, NY 10016

Library of Congress Cataloging-in-Publication Data

Patterson, Jerry L.
  Break the dealer.

  Bibliography: p.
  1. Blackjack (Game)   2. Gambling—United States.
3. Casinos—United States.   I. Olsen, Eddie.   II. Title.
GV1295.B55P385   1986   795.4′2   86-8104
ISBN 0-399-51233-0

Printed in the United States of America
         9   10

Contents

Introduction

Eddie Olsen and I are both successful professional blackjack players. Between the two of us, we've played an estimated 1.1 million hands of casino blackjack since 1979. During the course of our play, we have carefully observed the changes that have come about in the game, particularly since the abolishment of "early surrender"—a blackjack option available to Atlantic City players until 1982. The changes have been subtle—but they have had a devastating impact on a player's ability to win at the game. In *Break the Dealer: Winning Strategies for Today's Blackjack,* we bring you up-to-date on those changes and teach you the new techniques you must know in order to be a winner in blackjack as it exists *today*.

The problem with many of the blackjack books currently on the market is that they are a rehash of techniques that were developed years ago, and address a game that, in some respects, no longer exists. Casinos have changed the number of decks used in most of the games. They have effectively reduced the betting spread. And, perhaps most important of all, they have introduced new shuffling procedures in order to influence the kind of cards that are dealt; yes, they can even manipulate a player's chances of winning or losing in many instances. In *Break the Dealer,* we fully describe the new shuffling procedures and explain how to detect and exploit them. Many of the strategies and techniques in *Break the Dealer* have never before been published. Developed by Eddie and me, they have been proven in countless sessions of casino blackjack, and successfully used by us and our students. In addition to describing shuffling procedures designed by casino operators and industry consultants to beat blackjack players, we will show you:

• The methods some dealers use to stop winning players—and how to combat such tactics.
• New tools of the game.
• How to select winning games before sitting down at a table.
• How to prolong a favorable game with the cut card—the most overlooked tool in blackjack.
• A mental conditioning program designed to improve table discipline.
• Special money-management strategies for both the Nevada and Atlantic City games.

We will also introduce special drills that we have developed to hone the more traditional blackjack tools—basic strategy and card counting. Many of these drills have been used to train and develop more than 10,000 successful blackjack players throughout the world.

This book reflects six years of research on the part of Eddie and me, as well as interviews with casino presidents, pit personnel, dealers, shuffling-machine inventors, computer scientists, casino-industry consultants, and blackjack "personalities." *Break the Dealer* is bound to provoke controversy among state agencies, casino executives, and our blackjack colleagues. We welcome your reactions. In the meantime, read, study, enjoy—and learn how to become a winner!

JERRY L. PATTERSON

BREAK THE DEALER

1 Changing Times

Appearances are deceptive.

—AESOP

Blackjack has always been a popular casino game because of the fact that players have always felt the game could be beaten. In 1962, Edward O. Thorp, a professor of mathematics at the University of California, confirmed this belief in his groundbreaking book, *Beat the Dealer,* when he showed that it was indeed possible to gain a mathematical advantage over a casino by using basic strategy and card counting.

Since then, an increasing number of players have developed skills that enable them to win at blackjack. Some, in fact, have even made blackjack their profession; others play semiprofessionally. Skilled players, however, represent only a tiny fraction of the total blackjack market. For the great majority of people who play, blackjack remains a game of chance. Nevertheless, over the years, casino operators have grown afraid of the game because of losses, sometimes significant ones, to a few skilled players. Casino operators don't seem to realize that these losses have helped their industry more than they have harmed it from a promotional standpoint. The fact that blackjack can be beaten

13

makes it the most attractive of the casino games and draws business to the casinos. The industry has in fact thrived with blackjack as its flagship. In 1983, blackjack earned roughly $1.8 billion—more than 75 percent—of the total $2.3 billion earned by Nevada casinos from table games. And in 1984, blackjack accounted for about 50 percent, or $446 million, of $891 million earned from Atlantic City table games. Blackjack has been the bread and butter of the gaming industry's growth in both Nevada and New Jersey.

Nonetheless, the industry remains uneasy with blackjack because it does not have fixed odds. Casino operators fear there may be a growing number of players capable of exploiting the game, nibbling into their profits. Unlike blackjack, other casino games *do* have fixed odds—odds as high as 25 percent in favor of the house. Games with fixed odds produce reasonably predictable earnings. Blackjack, with its lack of fixed odds, makes for unpredictability. And unpredictability makes casino operators nervous. As Larry Woolf, former vice-president of operations at Caesars Boardwalk Regency in Atlantic City, and presently president of Caesars Taho in Nevada, puts it, "Many people liken casinos to public institutions, like lending libraries. We're a private business and must make a profit to stay in business. If we lose money in, say, blackjack, then we must remedy that . . . doing away with it, if necessary."

Bill Friedman, president of the Castaways Hotel/Casino and the Silver Slipper Casino in Las Vegas, writes in his book, *Casino Management,* that a surprising number of executives cannot stand to see the casino lose. Not even a single table. These "bleeders," or "sweaters," as Friedman characterized them, will often attempt to increase the table-hold percentage—a win rate based on cash received and chips lost—at a table after several players have won by ordering the dealers to speed up the games, "even though it can offend and drive away customers."

Not everyone agrees that this is a good practice. One former pit boss, and later a distinguished player, when asked if he became nervous if a table was losing money, replied, "Heck no. When a blackjack game was unloading [when a table was losing], I just let it go; it was good for business. The players had to win sometimes, too."

But for the New Era casino executives, managing a casino correctly means gambling with as little risk as possible. One longtime Las Vegas resident summed it up best: "The trouble with most of the corporations is that they aren't gamblers; they don't like to lose."

Casinos and casino blackjack have been changing in America for a long time. From 1931 until 1978, Nevada was the only state in the union where gambling was legal. Will Rogers congratulated the citizens of Nevada in 1931 for making gambling legal, and "shaking off the cloak of hypocrisy" that existed in other areas where illegal gambling ran rampant. Still, for forty-seven years investors and bankers were reluctant to consider the gambling industry anything more than a "shady enterprise" and big corporations by and large refused to have any part of it. In 1978, Atlantic City changed all that by becoming the second area of the country to offer legalized gambling. Atlantic City, with its close proximity to New York's Wall Street, helped attract big-name corporations to the gaming industry. As gambling became more socially acceptable, and as the gambling houses were bought up by corporations, the old-style casinos disappeared.

Gone from the business today are the likes of Harold Smith and his father, Pappy, who created a carnival-like atmosphere at Harolds Club at Reno's famed Virginia Street. Whenever they were on the casino floor dealing blackjack—and they were, occasionally—winners were paid double.

Another innovator and maverick, now gone, was William Fisk Harrah, who began with a simple bingo parlor in Reno, later moved to a bar with one blackjack table, and went on to build a casino-hotel empire founded on his uncompromising insistence on perfection in his hotel rooms and a favorable shuffle at his blackjack tables. Harrah's personal touch disappeared after he died in 1978 and the organization was absorbed by Holiday Inns, Inc.

The last of the great casino families today is headed by Benny Binion, the eighty-one-year-old patriarch of the Horseshoe Club in Las Vegas, the last old-time gambling hall in America. Binion, a former professional gambler himself, has accepted bets as high as $1 million. With a favorable single-deck game, the Horseshoe Club does wall-to-wall business the year round.

But the modern casino executive is quite unlike the old-time gambling-hall operator. The ten-gallon hat and chewing tobacco have been replaced by a three-piece suit and filtered low-tar cigarettes. What's more, the modern casino executive is more likely to be an Ivy League graduate and a subscriber to *The Wall Street Journal* than a former pit boss and reader of *Gambling Times* magazine. As family enterprises have given way to business giants like Hilton Hotels Corporation and Bally Manufacturing Corp., blackjack conditions have also undergone significant changes—changes that directly affect your ability to win at today's game.

Conditions for the traditional blackjack player—players who play basic strategy and count cards—were reasonably good in Atlantic City until September 1982, when New Jersey casinos could no longer bar card counters, due to a decision rendered the previous May by the state supreme court. The court's decision resulted from a suit filed by Ken Uston, a professional player, who, along with his teammates, was barred from Resorts International after they had won $145,000 during one nine-day period. During the first four years in Atlantic City, casinos barred nearly two thousand people as suspected card counters. Specially trained casino personnel, wary of anyone who even appeared knowledgeable of the game, went to great lengths to protect casino interests. One nonprofessional player described his experience when a casino suspected him of counting cards: "I was surrounded by four huge guys who told me, 'If you sit down again, we're going to throw you out bodily.' They started getting pretty nasty and I was treated like some sort of criminal."

In describing Ken Uston in 1981, Joel Sterns, attorney for Resorts International, said, "We consider Uston every bit as undesirable as a drunk or disorderly person."

Uston, when he filed his suit, became a national folk hero to the public. He represented "the little guy." In February 1981, Uston's case was examined on *Sixty Minutes*.

"Basically," Uston told interviewer Harry Reasoner, "I'm just using skill in a casino. I'm not cheating. I'm not doing anything other than trying to use my brain. And the fact that I'm not allowed to play bothers me. It would be as if Bobby Fischer is not allowed to play chess, or Pete Rose isn't allowed to play baseball, or Charles Goren isn't allowed to play bridge . . . sort of against the American way."

The New Jersey Supreme Court agreed with Uston and decided that suspected card counters could not be excluded by the casinos in the absence of a New Jersey Casino Control Commission regulation authorizing exclusion. The Casino Control Commission refused to implement such a regulation. Card counters could no longer be barred. Instead, the commission opted for a six-month period of testing and statistical analysis of games with various shuffles, rules, and procedures. The New Jersey casino operators reacted by creating monstrosities that ranged from eight-deck games to an experimental atrocity called Blackjack II, a twelve-deck game. In effect, they attempted to take the blackjack out of blackjack.

It was during this period that the present Atlantic City game was born. First, "early surrender" was eliminated; it had been a rule offered only in Atlantic City whereby blackjack players could, upon viewing their first two cards and the dealer's up-card, "surrender" instead of continuing play. Players who "surrendered" forfeited only half of their bet. The rule, favorable to the players, reduced the house advantage by .62 percent. The casinos unanimously did away with the option in 1982. Second, and much more important, the casinos began experimenting with different shuffles, in order to influence the card patterns and make the game more unfavorable to the players.

Last, the "wash"—a procedure in which new cards are opened, strewn onto the blackjack table, and intermixed for the purpose of mixing the decks—was cleverly manipulated by some casinos to achieve certain card patterns and increase the house advantage. The procedures—simple, subtle, and sophisticated—took advantage of traditional card-company packaging methods (ace to king in one suit, king to ace in the next) in which 50 percent of a deck's ten-value cards and aces are mated in a ten-card clump in the middle of each new deck. It was found that a series of "mini-washes" would even *increase* the clumping of similar cards. Perhaps as a result, most casinos discontinued "full washes," washes in which all of the decks are intermixed simultaneously. A casino with an eight-deck game, for example, could achieve greater clumping by spreading and crimping two decks at a time. The remaining decks would be processed in an identical manner. They then concluded the procedure with a circular mix and shuffle. Although this new procedure more than tripled the "down time"—time a dealer is not taking bets—required by the old "full wash," a statistical analysis of the new house win rates justified the longer method.

"Caesars' shuffle at the beginning of each shift is devastating to the counter," Uston wrote in his newsletter. "Cards of similar denomination and suit tend to stay together. I lost about $15,000 to the first shoe of the day shift as I watched all the low hearts dealt, followed by spades.

"I called over a [Casino Control] Commission official and had him observe the first shoe at another table. In the third round, of seven cards exposed, there was a royal flush in clubs. Card counting depends upon the random ordering of the cards. Clumping such as this will obliterate the counter."

This, in essence, is the general way in which casinos have managed to manipulate and change, forever, the game of blackjack. *All* previous blackjack strategies have been based on the notion of a random distribution of the cards. If the cards are *not* randomly distributed, the effectiveness of all existing blackjack strategies has been compromised and even rendered useless.

Excessive clumping resulting from inadequately "washed" cards can be encouraged and prolonged by sophisticated shuffling procedures. These procedures have been incorporated in Nevada games since at least 1979. Atlantic City began to use them following the Uston court decision. Since then, shuffles have been continuously modified with the sole purpose of subverting mathematical systems used to gain an advantage in blackjack. As one casino-industry veteran admits, "Some shuffles promote nonrandomness better than others."

In the past twenty-five years, blackjack has evolved from a simple game of chance to a highly sophisticated contest between casinos and blackjack players. Old values, such as the placement of the burn card and the mathematical strategies of card play, are not necessarily as relevant as they once were. To win in today's combative climate, blackjack players must be more observant, creative, and open-minded than yesterday's straight card counters. Casino managers today are much more knowledgeable about how to market and operate the game than they once were. As casinos have striven for higher profits, management has discovered better techniques to control the game. Today's New Era player must learn those techniques as well in order to successfully compete.

Break the Dealer is the first book to deal with the new shuffles and the game of blackjack as it now exists. It goes beyond theoretical or textbook blackjack to include the casino conditions as they exist today. Despite the changes in the game, *it is possible to win at blackjack—if you know how*. In fact, there are advantages today unique to both Atlantic City and Nevada. In Atlantic City, for example:

- Card counters—or winning players suspected of being card counters—can no longer be barred.
- Betting large amounts of money (green chips worth $25, black $100 chips or purple $500 chips) does not attract the negative attention that it does in most Nevada houses. Bigger betting spreads are possible.

• Atlantic City is easier to cover or scout than Las Vegas, because virtually all casinos are concentrated in one of two areas. In Las Vegas, the casinos and clubs are scattered; it is not feasible to cover the city on foot.

• Because of a state law requiring that all cards be dealt from a shoe, rather than a dealer's hand, the chances of being cheated in Atlantic City are remote.

Nevada, however, has many other advantages:

• There is more diversity in the types of games available throughout Nevada, because houses are not as stringently regulated by the state as they are in Atlantic City. Each house is free to choose the number of decks to be used for its games while establishing its own table minimums and blackjack rules. Consequently, single-deck blackjack, the most favorable game to the player, is offered throughout Nevada. Other games feature two decks and four decks as well as shoe games ranging from five to eight decks.

• Table minimums are generally lower in Nevada.

• Overall, more reasonable blackjack conditions—including favorable shuffles and fewer decks—make the Nevada games superior to the ones in Atlantic City.

• Aside from blackjack, food and lodging prices are as much as 60 percent lower in Nevada than in Atlantic City.

• The clubs and casinos are more calm and relaxed. In general, dealers are friendlier and more courteous.

We are not advocating that basic strategy and card counting be abandoned in today's game. They are *still important* in gaining an advantage over the casinos. To make a brief analogy, you have to learn how to walk before you can run. We will go over basic strategy and card counting in the following chapters, and show you their place in today's game. And we'll provide you with a number of never-before-published drills that will help you to master basic strategy and card counting within a reasonable period of time. But basic strategy and card counting, no matter how sophisticated and advanced, are *not enough* anymore to consistently win at today's game. Today's player, the New Era player, must be knowledgeable about shuffles as well. He or she must be able to distinguish between a favorable shuffle and an unfavorable shuffle—as well as how to exploit an unfavorable shuffle when it is offered. Only by understanding how the shuffle works, and how casinos manipulate the cards, can you expect to beat the shuffle and play profitable blackjack. So read on, and learn how to become not just a player, but a *winner*.

2 How Casinos Think

Whoever tries for great objects must suffer something.

—PLUTARCH

All blackjack games are not alike. Some houses offer games so one-sided you would be better off playing three-card monte on the streets of New York City. This is not a complaint. Casinos have every right to make their games as favorable or unfavorable as they wish, provided they do not cheat.

The purpose of this chapter is to show you how and why casinos make the decisions that they do, and the effect these decisions have on the blackjack games they offer.

Casino Management and Blackjack Marketing Strategies

Casino managers are able to manipulate and control the game of blackjack in primarily four ways. They are:

1. The number of decks to be used.

2. The type of shuffle (unbalanced, strip, zone, etc.).

3. The number of rounds to be dealt (the penetration of a deck).

4. The house rules (doubling down, surrendering, etc.).

All of these considerations have dollar values to the

casino that can be calculated and projected based on mathematics or past performance.

For example, a basic-strategy player has about a .1 percent advantage in a single-deck game. The house has about a .4 percent advantage when four or more decks are used. Today's managers—the New Era casino managers—know those statistical differences.

The New Era casino manager knows a single-deck game costs the house more than half a percent advantage in real dollars, because a single-deck game requires more manpower hours for surveillance and attracts more card counters.

Multiple-deck games can be made more attractive to blackjack players with liberal rules, such as allowing players to double down after splitting pairs (worth about .1 percent advantage). The casino manager often acts like a track handicapper in a sense, structuring games to correspond to the financial goals established by the house. If the goal is to attract more people into the casinos, the blackjack rules are amended to make the game more attractive to players. If the object is to increase the table-hold percentage—the amount of money a table brings in—they may tighten the rules and make the game less favorable to players.

When the house wants to increase its profits, and the casino manager is convinced there are no internal problems—such as cheating or pilfering—he will usually modify the shuffle. There are sophisticated data bases available on shuffles in which performance has been monitored and compared.

Imagine for a moment that you have been named casino manager at a major new resort hotel on the Strip in Las Vegas. Your position makes you the most powerful executive at the new resort, answerable only to the board of directors. The resort has two championship golf courses, modern health-spa facilities, and a youthful, upbeat image.

Obviously, you would gear the casino to the affluent or "premium" gambler instead of the "grinder," the player who buys in for $20 and bets $2 until the house "grinds" him out.

As casino manager, you might open with a four-deck game, using a zone shuffle with 1½ decks cut out of play and reasonable house rules. "Premiums" wouldn't reject the game and card-counter traffic would be within reason. Being the "new kid on the block," you would tell floor personnel to be patient with the games. No stripping. Introduce yourself to all high rollers, for they are your most desirable customers. Promote the resort's facilities. If your restaurant is moderately priced, be liberal with complimentary service. Smile. Gather names for the computer. Your priority is to make your customers want to come back again and again. Remind the dealers to smile.

Let's examine a different marketing strategy, an exaggerated situation that you aren't likely to find today, but may have found in 1979.

You have been named casino manager at a club in downtown Las Vegas. Besides slot machines and a craps table, there's a snack bar and six blackjack tables. Your boss has given you the word: Things are tight, baby.

In this case, you might open with one single-deck game at the rear of the club, one two-deck game, and four six-deck games. One single-deck game is all you need to advertise "single-deck 21" on your marquee. The minimum bet would be $1, and 50 percent of the tables would be closed during nonpeak periods. For the single-deck and two-deck games, the house shuffle would be unbalanced with double-stripping. The shuffle used in shoe games would be a zone shuffle with stripping. (Note: Both will be discussed in later chapters; both are unfavorable shuffles to blackjack players.)

Cultivate locals, give them a break now and then. Beat the out-of-towners. Shorten the games (reduce the number of rounds dealt per deck) against anyone who poses a threat. (This reduces the opportunity for card counters to exploit a high count in a deck.) Police the games carefully because security will be light (no staffing on weekdays) in the sky overhead. Question shift losses; "sweat" every hand. Encourage liberal use of "shills"—players hired by the house to create a busy appearance. Pay them $20 a day with free alcoholic drinks (it doesn't matter if they are sober). Watch out for cheating dealers. Promote and demote. Use scratch-and-claw psychology.

Obviously, the long-term prospects for this house aren't bright. With its limited bankroll, it should be in the laundry or fast-food business, not the casino business.

Now, let's take a third situation: a casino which is both profitable and which offers a favorable or forthright shuffle. Binion's Horseshoe Club in Las Vegas. This casino has thirty-two blackjack tables, twenty-seven of which offer single-deck games; four offer two-deck games; and one offers a four-deck game. The house shuffle is a forthright shuffle, with no stripping. This casino does not fear winning players. It is, truly, in the gambling business. It also has the house percentage on its side because most players play until they lose, no matter how much they win. Even if they leave as winners, they come back later and lose. The attitude toward card counters is be reasonable with them but don't let them abuse the house. Once when we played at Binion's, a floor person whispered to one of our players, who attempted a 5-1 spread, "Keep your betting spread to 4-1 and we'll gamble with you." If you are fair and reasonable with the dealers, they'll be fair and reasonable with you.

"Let's just put it this way," owner Benny Binion told *The Wall Street Journal,* "we got a little joint and a big bankroll, and all them others got a big joint and a little bankroll." They have the highest business volume in the state as a result.

The Horseshoe Club is a textbook case of blackjack marketing and casino psychology. They try to foster business. For example, if a player bets five red chips (worth $5 each) and wins, the payoff is made with five red chips instead of one green chip (worth $25). The chips on the table are good advertising and an incentive to gamble more money.

Although Horseshoe Club officials declined to discuss their blackjack profits, an authoritative source said their table hold (a profit indicator) averages between 9 and 13 percent. In the 1980's, blackjack table holds have been as high as 29.2 percent on the Las Vegas Strip, 20.7 percent in downtown Las Vegas, 26.2 percent at Reno, 31.8 percent at Lake Tahoe, and 17.4 percent in Atlantic City. So the Horseshoe Club, in comparison, has a low table hold.

But consider business volume. Would you rather have a small piece of $1.1 million or a larger piece of $124,000? Nine percent of $1.1 million is $99,000 compared to 31.8 percent of $124,000 for a gross profit of $39,432.

Until 1980, casinos traditionally marketed to either "premiums" or "grinders"—the high and the low end. Interestingly enough, Atlantic City and a new Eastern attitude toward casino gambling have fostered a new market—the middle-income American.

How a Casino Sees Itself Can Affect Its Blackjack Policies

John F. Chiero, president and general manager of the Tropicana in Las Vegas, is implementing a renovation that includes a five-acre tropical island, five lagoons, a 41,000-

square-foot convention center, and a twenty-two-story tower with 806 additional rooms. What the Tropicana project represents is a redefinition of its marketing image from a casino-hotel to a convention-center/resort-hotel, a trend started by the MGM Grand Hotel in Las Vegas (now known as Bally's Grand).

"We consider ourselves basically a convention hotel and the casino part of the entertainment package for conventions," said the MGM's Stephen Allen in 1985. "Consequently, convention business is what we are trying to attract rather than that of the card counter."

MGM's five-deck game with a zone shuffle and stripping was no award-winner, as far as players are concerned. But the hotel won a number of awards from various trade publications as a premier convention facility. There was no reason for the MGM to showcase a favorable blackjack game as long as there are conventioneers to fill the tables, no questions asked. This is an example of *reverse marketing*.

Casino Conditions Today

The number of single-deck and two-deck games in Las Vegas declined by 9 percent in 1980. Card-counter traffic declined and so did casino profits. Some Las Vegas operators blamed the slump on Atlantic City.

"I didn't think it would take as much away from our market," Binion told *Las Vegas Today* during a 1980 interview. "I and others misjudged it."

While Atlantic City may have been a factor in the Las Vegas slump, we feel the growing number of unfavorable multiple-deck games also contributed to that slump. Six-deck games represented only 14 percent of the games offered in 1979, but increased to 37 percent in 1983. Single-deck games declined from 21 percent to 9 percent during the same period. Las Vegas was no longer America's gaming capital; it had evolved into a West Coast version of Atlantic City. And a five-year comparision of the blackjack games underscores that trend:

GAMES ON THE LAS VEGAS STRIP

Year	1-Deck	2-Deck	4-Deck	5-Deck	6-Deck
1979.......	21%	26%	36%	2%	15%
1983.......	8%	20%	16%	21%	35%

GAMES IN DOWNTOWN LAS VEGAS

Year	1-Deck	2-Deck	4-Deck	5-Deck	6-Deck*
1979.......	19%	42%	22%	4%	13%
1983.......	14%	25%	16%	2%	43%

*Includes 7-deck games.

In 1983, Las Vegas suffered a recession. The recession alarmed casino operators because Las Vegas had always considered itself the world's only "recession-proof" city. Profits at the major houses dropped a staggering 42 percent—from $315 million in 1982 to $180.5 million.

Furthermore, the industry was stunned when the Riviera Hotel & Casino became the first major resort on the Las Vegas Strip to seek protection from creditors under Chapter 11 of the Federal Bankruptcy Act. Several other houses would follow, including the Aladdin Hotel & Casino, the Marina Hotel & Casino, the Landmark Hotel Casino, and the Dunes Hotel and Casino.

As a result, many houses tightened operations even more. But shrewd casino operators revived single-deck and two-deck games. The enticement paid off; the card counters returned. But this time, casino operators were ready for them with countermeasures, "game-control" techniques, and, finally, thoughtful marketing strategies.

The Countermeasures

One of the most effective countermeasures employed against suspected card counters is "breaking the deck." The dealer simply reshuffles the cards whenever a player substantially increases a bet. Floor personnel and dealers are now more sensitive than ever to betting spreads of three-to-one or more, particularly in hand-held games (games where the dealer deals from his or her hand).

The most popular deterrent to card counters has been the multiple-deck game, which originated in the Caribbean casinos. Operators favored multiple-deck games because they reduced shuffle time and statistically increased the house advantage.

Later, casino operators learned that insufficiently shuffled shoe games increased the house advantage even more.

Changing markets, new competitors, and increased conservatism within the industry, perhaps encouraged by an influx of hotel-management executives, inspired many executives to turn to the computer for assistance; others sought professional consultants specializing in casino-industry-related problems. Some casinos even resorted to employing the services of Griffin Investigators, Inc., a Las Vegas–based firm that gathers and distributes descriptions and photographs of suspected card counters as well as cheating players and casino employees.

The scientific or New Era casino operator had slouched to Las Vegas (and Atlantic City) to be born.

New Era Casino Operators

In 1979, casino management was not particularly concerned with unoccupied rooms or food-and-beverage deficits as long as gambling revenue paid the bills. This is no longer true. New Era casino operators expect all of their divisions to contribute to the bottom line. Their styles reflect two common touches: accountability and profit-ability.

While blackjack is still one of the gambling industry's most attractive products (blackjack earnings eclipsed all other Nevada table games combined in 1980), New Era casino operators have learned that single-deck and two-deck games do not have to be offered year-round or casino-wide; they can be effective "bait" at a handful of tables on a seasonal basis.

"Game-Control" Methods

"Game-control" measures are designed to protect the house bankroll. They may or may not have an impact on a game and should serve as a signal that the house is making an extra effort to beat you.

"Game-control" measures should not be confused with countermeasures, which are designed specifically as a deterrent to card counters. "Game-control" measures are intended as a deterrent to winning players. We talked with former casino managers, pit bosses, dealers, industry consultants, and operators of dealers' schools in order to learn about "game-control" measures. The most effective methods are discussed here:

The Strip Shuffle. Particularly effective in the single-deck game, the strip shuffle may increase "stiff hands" (two-card totals of 12 through 16)—otherwise known as losing hands—by as much as 15 percent, according to two unaffiliated owners of dealers' schools.

June D., a former Reno dealer, said she was taught the strip shuffle at the Cal Neva Club because the house was sensitive to "*anyone* winning." She also dealt single-deck blackjack at Harrah's, the Money Tree, and the Mapes Hotel. "If you wanted to keep working, you had to learn how to keep the game under control," June D. said. "Some casinos did not mind the players winning as much as others."

Insufficiently Shuffled Cards. Used in both single-deck and multiple-deck games, a light shuffle with a fresh deck may have originated with old-time casino operators who had a saying, "Cards that aren't shuffled can't be beaten." An unbalanced shuffle will promote insufficient shuffling in a single-deck game. Frequent changing of cards may accomplish the same result. Ironically, Ken Uston, in his 1977 book, *The Big Player,* wrote: "There is the possibility . . . that when new cards are brought into play, the house advantage can be increased through inadequate shuffling of the new deck, which results in the clumping of identical cards."

One industry consultant, the president of a computer firm, said insufficiently shuffled cards give the house an additional advantage over skillful players. He said he has researched both six-deck and eight-deck shuffling techniques.

Plugging the Shoe. A relatively new technique for thwarting players tracking the shuffle and "location bettors," plugging the shoe is common in many multiple-deck games. It involves taking unplayed cards, dividing them into three or more stacks, and randomly inserting them among the remaining cards prior to the shuffle.

Preferential Shuffling. A method that can increase the house advantage by as much as 29 percent, preferential shuffling requires the dealer to keep track of the cards as a card counter would do, shuffling when the deck becomes favorable to the players.

In 1979, Stanley R. Sludikoff, publisher of *Gambling Times* magazine, documented one example of preferential shuffling when he obtained confidential shuffling instructions for dealers at the Jolly Trolley Casino in Las Vegas.

The instructions threatened possible suspension and termination for failure to comply. Dealers were required to shuffle anytime a total of six 4s, 5s, and 6s was placed in the discard rack.

Old or Soft Cards. It is possible that using soft or worn cards, combined with a favorable shuffle, can increase the house's advantage. However, we have not been able to substantiate this theory.

Dishonest Casino Operators

Since 1979, we have been unable to corroborate a single report alleging a cheating dealer or house. Casino personnel that we interviewed said it is unlikely for any house to risk the loss of its license simply to beat a player.

In the past, typical forms of cheating that have reportedly taken place include:

Stacking the deck (the prearrangement of cards in a particular order to favor the house).

Reversing the deck (dealing cards that have been previously dealt in a hand-held game).

Shorting the deck (removing cards favorable to the players, such as 10s or aces).

Dealing "seconds" (giving a player the second card from the top of the deck when the values of the top card and the dealer's hole card are known).

False shuffling (simulating a shuffle, but not intermixing the cards, to preserve a clump of cards).

State investigators in both New Jersey and Nevada said one of the most frequent problems is dealers in collusion with other players to cheat the house. In fact, Nevada Attorney General Brian McKay said some "gangs" have used "Star Wars" techniques, utilizing such equipment as computers, zoom cameras, infrared binoculars, transmitters, and even laser guns.

Regulatory Control of Blackjack

In Nevada, Gaming Division regulators appear to be interested only in keeping the games honest and making sure everyone pays his bills. In New Jersey, casino executives have privately complained about excessive state controls and dictatorial policies that have caused building plans to be redesigned and the color of bathroom tiles to be altered.

Business analyst Lee S. Isgur of Paine Webber, Inc., blamed regulatory authorities for sluggishness at every level of the Atlantic City market. "When I look at Atlantic City, I do not see much difference between the various casinos," Isgur told *Gaming & Wagering Business* magazine. "It appears that it is almost mandatory to have an ice-cream parlor, a steak house, an Italian restaurant, and, of course, a Japanese or Chinese restaurant."

State controls have encouraged conformity in the table games. So much so that John Gallaway, president of the Tropicana Hotel & Casino in Atlantic City, was reluctant to introduce an experimental four-deck game in 1984 without first seeking the Casino Control Commission's endorsement as a "courtesy" measure. With the exception of the Tropicana's four-deck game, the only imaginative marketing programs that developed between 1982 and 1985 were geared for busing programs and slot-machine players.

Besides being policymakers, New Jersey regulators are also business partners in a sense, since state income is derived from casino profits. That partnership was particularly evident in 1981 when the Casino Control Commission issued an economic "emergency" waiver to eliminate blackjack's "early-surrender" rule after four of seven casinos reported losses.

Researchers George Sternlieb and James W. Hughes,

in their book, *The Atlantic City Gamble,* characterized the use of such power as "startling." *The Wall Street Journal* noted that the declaration of an economic emergency enabled the commission to act without a formal public hearing. The commission overstepped its authority and former Governor Brendan Byrne finally declared the appropriate emergency.

Since 1981, one profit indicator, the blackjack table hold, has increased from 13 percent to 17 percent in New Jersey casinos. This has occurred despite the fact that the mathematical value of "early surrender" favored the player by .62 percent. What's more, card counters have been allowed to play since September 15, 1982, and earnings have not declined; they increased. To ensure those profits, the Casino Control Commission authorized a number of countermeasures and "game-control" options.

The options included:

Cutting as many as 50 percent of the cards out of play.

Various continuous shuffling procedures, including the Bart Carter Shuffle and Resorts Continuous Shuffle II.

An experimental game called Blackjack II, a twelve-deck game dealt from a double shoe.

Limiting table maximums to as little as $100.

Restricting the wagering of new players to the table minimum.

These options were part of a six-month program of experimental games and field testing authorized by the Casino Control Commission to "assure maximum patron participation, fair odds as well as the economic viability of the industry." The commission also considered massive rules changes that would have made the Atlantic City game unpopular.

The rules weren't changed. The Bart Carter Shuffle, Blackjack II, and other experimental games disappeared.

Wagering wasn't permanently restricted. The industry opted for an "invisible deterrent" to card counters—shuffling procedures that inhibit distribution. Blackjack profits increased. Many traditional card counters left town. And the New Era player—armed with new techniques to beat the game—was born.

This, then, is the blackjack scene today. Now let's look at the various tools and techniques that have been developed to beat today's game.

3 Basic Strategy

Mathematics possesses not only truth, but supreme beauty—a beauty cold and austere, like that of sculpture, without appeal to any part of our weaker nature. . . .
                                                                —BERTRAND RUSSELL

"Basic strategy" is a mathematically developed method for playing blackjack that increases a player's chances of winning. In casino blackjack, the casino, or "house," holds about a 6-percent advantage over players who do not incorporate card counting, basic strategy, or other blackjack methods or strategies. This means that on the average, the house will win 53 percent of all hands played. The house advantage is due to the fact that the dealer always plays last. Any player who "breaks"—someone whose hand exceeds 21—immediately loses his bet, regardless of what happens during the dealer's play. By incorporating basic strategy, however, a player can increase the chances of winning while reducing the house advantage to about .6 percent. By using *both* basic strategy and card counting, a player can actually gain an advantage of at least 1 percent over the house. Learning basic strategy is as essential a fundamental tool to winning at blackjack as learning arithmetic is to learning to become a banker.

Outside Atlantic City—in Nevada, the Bahamas, Monte Carlo—basic strategy varies from house to house, depending on the rules and the number of decks dealt. But in Atlantic City, because the rules are the same, regardless of the casino, and because the number of decks used is relatively standard (all games feature four or more decks), basic strategy is always the same.

Basic strategy originated back in the early 1950s, when four mathematicians in the U.S. Army—Roger Baldwin, Wilbert Cantey, Herbert Maisel, and James Mc-Dermott—used desktop calculators to devise a way to significantly reduce the house advantage in blackjack by calculating the best possible play in most blackjack situations. Their calculations were published in the *Journal of the American Statistical Association* in 1956. These calculations were subsequently revised, and improved upon, following high-speed computer studies by Edward O. Thorp. Thorp's basic strategy was later given additional refinements by Julian H. Braun of IBM that actually gave the player a .1-percent advantage over the house. Using the computer, these men played thousands of hands for each possible blackjack situation and determined the best play for each hand, statistically. If, for example, a player has a hand totaling 16 and the dealer has a 4 up-card, the best possible play is to stand and not take another card. Granted, 16 is generally a losing hand—you will lose more often than you will win with it. Basic strategy cannot change that. But by deciding to stand, you figure to win about 40 percent of the time, while if you "hit," or take another card, you would win only 29 percent of the hands. Statistically, you will win *more often*—a gain of about 22 percent (11 percent more wins and 11 percent fewer losses)—by making the play that basic strategy dictates in this particular situation.

Some basic-strategy players do not always make the play they're supposed to make. Such is the case with "Blackjack Annie," a New Jersey friend. Frequently, she'll make a play variation for no particular reason. In one game, Blackjack Annie stood with a hard 16 against the dealer's up-card of 7. (A hard 16 is a two-card hand that totals 16 without an ace, which can be counted as either 1 or 11. A soft hand is a two-card hand with an ace. "I just hate that hand," Blackjack Annie would say later. "I usually hit it, but I had a hunch that I was going to break." (To hit is to decide to take another card. You may hit as long as you don't have 21. To break is to go over 21.)

Basic-strategy players must play every hand perfectly if they hope to break even or make a slight profit. Often, the difference between winning and losing is one hand— or one mistake. Players like Blackjack Annie must ignore their hunches and make the correct play on *every* hand. They must accept the fact that they'll be getting mediocre hands—hard two-card totals of 12 through 17—about 42 percent of the time. If Blackjack Annie always remembers to hit a hard 16 against a 7, her long-term gain could be as high as 7 percent.

Here are a few other hands that often confuse inexperienced players:

- A,7 (soft 18) against the dealer's 9 up-card.
- A,7 against a dealer's 10.
- Hard 16 against a 10.

The correct basic strategy play for all three hands is to hit. With a 10 showing, statistically, the dealer will make a 20 or more about 41 percent of the time. By hitting a soft 18, the player may be dealt an ace, 2, or 3 and dramatically improve the hand. A 10 would make the hand a hard 18 and a 9 would make it a hard 17. Only five cards—4, 5, 6, 7, and 8—would make the hand less than 17, but then the player would still have another chance to improve it by taking another card.

We have provided you with five basic-strategy charts in this chapter. The first one, "Basic Strategy for the Atlantic City Game (Multi-Deck)," is the only one you need to master for playing blackjack in Atlantic City casinos. Two of the remaining charts apply to basic strategy in Las Vegas: one for single-deck play and one for multi-deck play. The fourth basic-strategy chart is for the single-deck game as it is played in northern Nevada, outside of Las Vegas. The column on the extreme left of these charts indicates your hand as it has been dealt. The numbers at the top of the charts indicate the dealer's up-card. The symbols used within the charts stand for the four possible types of play: to hit (H), or take another card; to stand (S), or hold with the cards you have been dealt; to double down (D), or double the bet you made before being dealt your first two cards (remember, when you double down, you are allowed to receive only *one* additional card—you do not have the option of being able to hit again); and to split (P), creating two hands from cards with identical value and making equal bets for each hand. The fifth chart, on page 45, is another way to present the basic strategy for the multi-deck Atlantic City game. This chart should prove much easier to memorize and recite.

In deciding whether to hit or stand, a basic-strategy player should think of the dealer's up-card in terms of low cards and high cards. Low cards are those with a face value of 2 through 6, and high cards are those with a face value of 7 or more. When the dealer's up-card is a low card, the basic-strategy player does not hit a breaking hand—a hand that totals more than 11. (An exception to

BASIC STRATEGY FOR THE ATLANTIC CITY GAME
(MULTI-DECK)

THE DEALER'S UP-CARD

YOUR HAND	2	3	4	5	6	7	8	9	10	A
8	H	H	H	H	H	H	H	H	H	H
9	H	D	D	D	D	H	H	H	H	H
10	D	D	D	D	D	D	D	D	H	H
11	D	D	D	D	D	D	D	D	D	H
12	H	H	S	S	S	H	H	H	H	H
13	S	S	S	S	S	H	H	H	H	H
14	S	S	S	S	S	H	H	H	H	H
15	S	S	S	S	S	H	H	H	H	H
16	S	S	S	S	S	H	H	H	H	H
17	S	S	S	S	S	S	S	S	S	S
A,2	H	H	H	D	D	H	H	H	H	H
A,3	H	H	H	D	D	H	H	H	H	H
A,4	H	H	D	D	D	H	H	H	H	H
A,5	H	H	D	D	D	H	H	H	H	H
A,6	H	D	D	D	D	H	H	H	H	H
A,7	S	D	D	D	D	S	S	H	H	H
A,8	S	S	S	S	S	S	S	S	S	S
A,9	S	S	S	S	S	S	S	S	S	S
A,A	P	P	P	P	P	P	P	P	P	P
2,2	P	P	P	P	P	P	H	H	H	H
3,3	P	P	P	P	P	P	H	H	H	H
4,4	H	H	H	P	P	H	H	H	H	H
6,6	P	P	P	P	P	H	H	H	H	H
7,7	P	P	P	P	P	P	H	H	H	H
8,8	P	P	P	P	P	P	P	P	P	P
9,9	P	P	P	P	P	S	P	P	S	S
10,10	S	S	S	S	S	S	S	S	S	S

H = Hit. S = Stand. D = Double Down. P = Split.

BASIC STRATEGY FOR THE LAS VEGAS GAME
(SINGLE-DECK)

THE DEALER'S UP-CARD

YOUR HAND	2	3	4	5	6	7	8	9	10	A
8	H	H	H	D	D	H	H	H	H	H
9	D	D	D	D	D	H	H	H	H	H
10	D	D	D	D	D	D	D	D	H	H
11	D	D	D	D	D	D	D	D	D	D
12	H	H	S	S	S	H	H	H	H	H
13	S	S	S	S	S	H	H	H	H	H
14	S	S	S	S	S	H	H	H	H	H
15	S	S	S	S	S	H	H	H	H	H
16	S	S	S	S	S	H	H	H	H	H
17	S	S	S	S	S	S	S	S	S	S
A,2	H	H	D	D	D	H	H	H	H	H
A,3	H	H	D	D	D	H	H	H	H	H
A,4	H	H	D	D	D	H	H	H	H	H
A,5	H	H	D	D	D	H	H	H	H	H
A,6	D	D	D	D	D	H	H	H	H	H
A,7	S	D	D	D	D	S	S	H	H	S
A,8	S	S	S	S	D	S	S	S	S	S
A,9	S	S	S	S	S	S	S	S	S	S
A,A	P	P	P	P	P	P	P	P	P	P
2,2	H	P	P	P	P	P	H	H	H	H
3,3	H	H	P	P	P	P	H	H	H	H
4,4	H	H	H	D	D	H	H	H	H	H
6,6	P	P	P	P	P	H	H	H	H	H
7,7	P	P	P	P	P	P	H	H	S	H
8,8	P	P	P	P	P	P	P	P	P	P
9,9	P	P	P	P	P	S	P	P	S	S
10,10	S	S	S	S	S	S	S	S	S	S

H = Hit. S = Stand. D = Double Down. P = Split.

BASIC STRATEGY FOR THE LAS VEGAS GAME
(MULTI-DECK)

THE DEALER'S UP-CARD

YOUR HAND	2	3	4	5	6	7	8	9	10	A
8	H	H	H	H	H	H	H	H	H	H
9	H	D	D	D	D	H	H	H	H	H
10	D	D	D	D	D	D	D	D	H	H
11	D	D	D	D	D	D	D	D	D	H
12	H	H	S	S	S	H	H	H	H	H
13	S	S	S	S	S	H	H	H	H	H
14	S	S	S	S	S	H	H	H	H	H
15	S	S	S	S	S	H	H	H	H	H
16	S	S	S	S	S	H	H	H	H	H
17	S	S	S	S	S	S	S	S	S	S
A,2	H	H	H	D	D	H	H	H	H	H
A,3	H	H	H	D	D	H	H	H	H	H
A,4	H	H	D	D	D	H	H	H	H	H
A,5	H	H	D	D	D	H	H	H	H	H
A,6	H	D	D	D	D	H	H	H	H	H
A,7	S	D	D	D	D	S	S	H	H	H
A,8	S	S	S	S	S	S	S	S	S	S
A,9	S	S	S	S	S	S	S	S	S	S
A,A	P	P	P	P	P	P	P	P	P	P
2,2	H	H	P	P	P	P	H	H	H	H
3,3	H	H	P	P	P	P	H	H	H	H
4,4	H	H	H	H	H	H	H	H	H	H
6,6	H	P	P	P	P	H	H	H	H	H
7,7	P	P	P	P	P	P	H	H	H	H
8,8	P	P	P	P	P	P	P	P	P	P
9,9	P	P	P	P	P	S	P	P	S	S
10,10	S	S	S	S	S	S	S	S	S	S

H = Hit. S = Stand. D = Double Down. P = Split.

BASIC STRATEGY FOR THE NORTHERN NEVADA GAME
(SINGLE-DECK)
THE DEALER'S UP-CARD

YOUR HAND	2	3	4	5	6	7	8	9	10	A
8	H	H	H	H	H	H	H	H	H	H
9	H	H	H	H	H	H	H	H	H	H
10	D	D	D	D	D	D	D	D	H	H
11	D	D	D	D	D	D	D	D	D	D
12	H	H	S	S	S	H	H	H	H	H
13	S	S	S	S	S	H	H	H	H	H
14	S	S	S	S	S	H	H	H	H	H
15	S	S	S	S	S	H	H	H	H	H
16	S	S	S	S	S	H	H	H	H	H
17	S	S	S	S	S	S	S	S	S	S
A,2	H	H	H	H	H	H	H	H	H	H
A,3	H	H	H	H	H	H	H	H	H	H
A,4	H	H	H	H	H	H	H	H	H	H
A,5	H	H	H	H	H	H	H	H	H	H
A,6	H	H	H	H	H	H	H	H	H	H
A,7	S	S	S	S	S	S	S	H	H	H
A,8	S	S	S	S	S	S	S	S	S	S
A,9	S	S	S	S	S	S	S	S	S	S
A,A	P	P	P	P	P	P	P	P	P	P
2,2	H	P	P	P	P	P	H	H	H	H
3,3	H	H	P	P	P	P	H	H	H	H
4,4	H	H	H	H	H	H	H	H	H	H
6,6	P	P	P	P	P	H	H	H	H	H
7,7	P	P	P	P	P	P	H	H	S	H
8,8	P	P	P	P	P	P	P	P	P	P
9,9	P	P	P	P	P	S	P	P	S	S
10,10	S	S	S	S	S	S	S	S	S	S

H = Hit. S = Stand. D = Double Down. P = Split.

BASIC STRATEGY FOR THE ATLANTIC CITY GAME
(MULTI-DECK)

Four-, Six-, or Eight-Deck

Your Hand	Rules for Dealer's Up-Cards
5 to 8	Always hit.
9	Double on 3 to 6. Otherwise hit.
10	Double on 2 to 9. Hit on 10, A.
11	Double on 2 to 10. Hit on A.
12	Stand on 4 to 6. Otherwise hit.
13	Stand on 2 to 6. Otherwise hit.
14	Stand on 2 to 6. Otherwise hit.
15	Stand on 2 to 6. Otherwise hit.
16	Stand on 2 to 6. Otherwise hit.
17	Always stand.
18 to 21	Always stand.
A,2	Double on 5, 6. Otherwise hit.
A,3	Double on 5, 6. Otherwise hit.
A,4	Double on 4 to 6. Otherwise hit.
A,5	Double on 4 to 6. Otherwise hit.
A,6	Double on 3 to 6. Otherwise hit.
A,7	Double on 3 to 6. Stand on 2, 7, or 8. Hit on 9, 10, or A.
A,8 to A,10	Always stand.
A,A	Always split.
2,2	Split on 2 to 7. Otherwise hit.
3,3	Split on 2 to 7. Otherwise hit.
4,4	Split on 5, 6. Otherwise hit.
5,5	Never split. Treat as 10, above.
6,6	Split on 2 to 6. Otherwise hit.
7,7	Split on 2 to 7. Otherwise hit.
8,8	Always split.
9,9	Split on 2 to 6, 8, or 9. Stand on 7, 10, or A.
10,10	Always stand.

this is when the dealer has an up-card of 2 or 3 and the basic-strategy player has a 12. In this case, the player would hit.) What is the reason for standing against most dealer low cards? When the dealer has a low card, the chances of the dealer breaking are dramatically higher. Computer studies show that when the dealer has an up-card of 5 or 6, for example, the chances of the dealer breaking are about 42 percent, or about 14 percent above normal. Over the long term, the dealer is expected to break 28 times out of every 100 hands, or about 28 percent. So the chances of a dealer breaking with a 5 or 6 showing are greatly enhanced. With a 4 up-card, the dealer should break about 39 percent of the time. In situations like this, you do not want to risk breaking yourself. It is statistically safer to stand, and hope the dealer breaks.

How does one learn basic strategy? You must memorize the chart or charts for the particular area you plan to play. There is no other way. You must practice until you no longer have to even think about making the correct decision. You must be able to make each play *automatically*. There are several drills on the following pages that can help you master basic strategy. Remember: You must not hesitate when making the correct basic-strategy play. You must double down or split whenever basic strategy dictates such a play. In doubling down, of course, you must double your bet, and you are permitted only one extra card. When basic strategy calls for such a play, it is because it is the *strongest possible* play. You must split when basic strategy calls for that play. Splitting means creating two hands out of a hand containing two like cards, such as two 3s or two 7s. This play permits you to bet two hands at once and works to your advantage under the proper circumstances. (Keep in mind, however, that when you split aces, most houses will allow only one card on each ace; you may not hit again.) Remember, too, that you never split 5s or 10s. A pair of 10s equals 20, which is always a standing hand. A pair of 5s is played as you would play a 10—hit if the dealer has a 10 or an ace; otherwise, double down.

The ace confuses many beginning players because it can be played as either a 1 or an 11. Blackjack Annie once stared a full thirty seconds at a soft 14, or ace-3 hand (a "soft" hand is one containing an ace, which may be played as either a 1 or an 11). The dealer had a 6 up-card. Biting her upper lip, she finally told the dealer her hand was "good"—in other words, she did not want to take another card. Later she confessed, "To be honest, I didn't know what to do."

Blackjack Annie not only missed a good double-down opportunity but also passed up an excellent chance of improving her hand. Only two cards—8 and 9—would have worsened it. A 10 would have given her a hard 14—the same value she stood with—and seven other cards would have improved her hand. By taking advantage of correct soft double downs, your game can be enhanced by as much as .14 percent. But keep in mind that some house rules—such as most single-deck games in Northern Nevada—do not allow soft double downs.

Surrender

Until 1982, Atlantic City casinos featured a rule that was unique—"early surrender." This rule enabled players to surrender, or throw in two-card hands after seeing the dealer's up-card, even if the up-card was an ace that subsequently resulted in a dealer blackjack. By "surrendering" their hands, players were given back half of their original bets. The rule improved the players' odds of winning by .62 percent, and attracted considerable attention and tourist business to Atlantic City. It was dropped when the casinos sought higher profits.

In a few Nevada casinos, variations of early surrender still exist. The most common form is called "late surrender." Late surrender allows players to take back half of their bets upon surrendering their two-card hands *after* the dealer has determined he or she does not have blackjack. If the dealer has blackjack, the player loses the entire bet.

When playing with four or more decks, the correct strategy is to late-surrender the following hands:

TWO-CARD HAND	TOTAL	DEALER'S UP-CARD
9,7	16	A
10,6*	16*	A
9,7*	16*	10
10,6*	16*	10
9,6*	15*	10
10,5*	15*	10
9,7	16	9
10,6	16	9

In a single-deck game, you would surrender only the above hands marked with an asterisk, as well as 7,7 against a dealer's 10 up-card.

Learning Aids

Learning basic strategy needn't be drudgery. In fact, it can be rather enjoyable and a good test of your imagination. First, examine and apply the accelerated learning techniques described elsewhere in this book. These techniques should prove helpful in learning basic strategy within a relatively short period of time. We also recommend using a variety of learning aids to make your drills as interesting as possible. The following do-it-yourself study aids should help you become a master of basic strategy in no time:

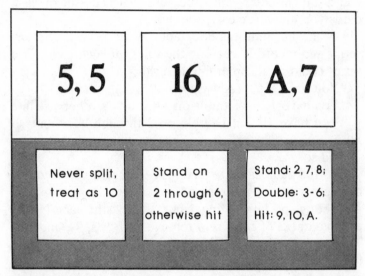

5, 5	16	A,7
Never split, treat as 10	Stand on 2 through 6, otherwise hit	Stand: 2, 7, 8; Double: 3-6; Hit: 9, 10, A.

Example of how homemade flash cards can be used as a learning tool for basic strategy. Write your hand on one side, the proper play on the other side.

• Make a set of flash cards, writing the player's two-card hand on one side and the correct play for that hand on the reverse side. Go through the cards, calling the play for each hand. Then check yourself. Put all the cards that stump you to one side and go through them again. Clock your efforts and compete for time, if you wish. Try first to leaf through the cards in two minutes. Once you are able to do that, shoot for ninety seconds. When you are able to whiz through the cards in less than one minute, you have mastered the drill. But remember: accuracy is even more important than speed. If you wish to learn more than one basic strategy (Atlantic City Multi-Deck, Las Vegas Single-Deck, etc.), be sure that each set of flash cards you make is clearly identified.

• Make an audiocassette tape. Write a basic-strategy script and record it, reciting the rules for each hand. The script could read something like this:

"You have 8 . . . Always hit.

"You have 9 . . . Double on 3 through 6, otherwise hit.

"You have 10 . . . Double on 2 through 9, otherwise hit."

And so on.

Play the audiocassette tape inside your car while you're on the road. Play the tape while you're asleep.

• Set up special training decks. For a "stiff-hand" drill, use two decks of cards and remove all 7s, 8s, 9s, and As. The majority of the hands will be "stiff hands"—two-card totals of 12, 13, 14, 15, or 16. Either use a low card or a high card as the dealer's up-card to make "hitting" and "standing" decisions. An alternative is to keep the player's hand constant—a 13, for example—and go through the deck varying the dealer's up-card.

For a "soft-double" drill, use two decks of cards and remove the 8s, 9s, and 10-value cards. Add 16 aces to the two decks. It is now designed to produce excessive "soft" hands (two-card combinations that include an ace). You can either deal yourself two cards and recite the appropriate rule, or deal a dealer's up-card as well and play out the hand. Soft hands are often difficult hands for the beginning player because of the dual value of the ace (it can be counted as either 1 or 11), and this drill should prove particularly helpful.

• Drill yourself using the basic-strategy drill included at

the end of the chapter. As you do the drill, stop and check yourself on any hand you're not sure about. Don't guess. Use the appropriate basic-strategy chart as a reference. Repeat the drill until you no longer have to refer to the chart.

Still another drill at the end of this chapter is a basic-strategy matrix in which you can write the play for each situation in abbreviated form. Use H for hit, S for stand, D for double, and P for split. Compete against the clock, if you wish. First, attempt to fill all the blanks in two minutes or less. Then try to improve on your time by thirty seconds. Keep practicing until you can complete the form in one minute or less. This is just one more drill to sharpen your skills and help you master basic strategy so that your responses are made automatically, without thinking.

• Finally, quiz yourself. Write all the two-hand combinations on a sheet of paper and include the rules for each hand. Don't peek and don't hurry. Grade and correct your effort.

Basic-Strategy Drill

Here are 126 blackjack hands. The player's hand is provided on the left and the dealer's up-card is on the right. Call each hand: hit (H), stand (S), double down (D), or split (P). If you're not sure, check the appropriate basic-strategy chart.

5,3 5	X,6 2	A,2 6	5,5 2	A,A 2	X,3 3	3,3 5
A,4 4	4,4 3	X,4 5	7,4 A	2,2 8	A,6 3	8,8 X
7,2 3	X,4 8	A,5 5	X,6 X	A,7 A	X,5 9	6,5 4
9,9 2	A,7 4	6,2 6	X,4 A	X,2 5	9,9 3	A,2 3
X,6 4	6,4 5	A,5 3	A,A A	7,7 5	X,4 4	7,4 2

A = ace. X = 10.

3,3 4	X,6 7	A,7 3	A,9 4	4,4 5	7,2 7	X,5 6
6,6 2	A,8 6	2,2 7	A,4 2	5,3 6	5,3 4	X,2 6
A,7 X	4,4 7	A,7 5	A,9 6	A,9 3	A,7 6	A,9 5
A,A 3	X,2 2	X,2 4	X,2 3	X,3 2	9,2 8	9,9 6
9,9 7	9,9 A	9,9 4	9,9 6	X,4 2	5,5 9	4,4 6
X,3 8	A,8 5	3,3 6	A,7 2	X,3 4	A,4 6	6,5 7
2,2 2	X,5 3	6,6 4	7,2 6	5,3 3	A,5 4	7,7 2
9,9 5	X,5 A	A,2 4	7,3 3	A,A 9	X,3 6	3,3 8
A,6 2	4,4 4	X,6 5	5,5 7	2,2 4	A,8 3	6,6 6
6,3 4	X,6 8	A,3 3	X,5 X	7,7 4	8,3 X	X,4 9
A,4 3	6,4 X	A,A X	X,5 5	3,3 3	A,6 6	6,2 5
X,4 3	8,3 9	2,2 6	A,3 5	6,6 7	5,4 8	X,3 5
3,3 7	4,4 2	7,7 8	X,6 6	7,3 8	8,8 9	7,3 A

A = ace. X = 10.

Basic-Strategy Matrix

In this drill, fill in the correct play for each hand, using H for hit, S for Stand, D for double down, and P for split. Fill in the correct play for each blank and grade your work against the appropriate basic-strategy chart. You may want to make extra copies of this matrix for future use before you get started.

DEALER'S UP-CARD

YOUR HAND	2	3	4	5	6	7	8	9	10	A
5–7										
8										
9										
10										
11										
12										
13										
14										
15										
16										
17–21										
A,2										
A,3										
A,4										
A,5										
A,6										
A,7										
A,8										
A,9										
A,A										
2,2										
3,3										
4,4										
5,5										
6,6										
7,7										
8,8										
9,9										
10,10										

4 Card Counting

*The race is not always to the swift, nor the battle to the strong—
but that's the way to bet.*

—DAMON RUNYON

Card counting is a technique for gathering information which can be used to determine advantage or disadvantage for betting purposes in games with a favorable shuffle.

Card counting also provides information for specific play variations and determines whether or not insurance should be taken. Card counting is an important basic tool for the player to use in combination with more advanced techniques—you will not win consistently just by counting cards.

Card counting is not fully understood, not even by many players who are serious about blackjack. Many novice players have turned away from blackjack because they put their total faith in card counting. The truth of the matter is that card counting is only a tool, no more significant than a rake or a shovel is to gardening. Card counting is an information-gathering technique that simply indicates the value of the unplayed cards or gives you some idea about the composition of the deck.

Card counting does not give you information about the distribution or lack of distribution among those unplayed cards. It is distribution, or the lack of distribution through the clumping of similar cards, that beats most players, whether they are card counters or not. Card counting works when there is randomness in the game. Randomness can only be achieved through a fair shuffle, or when all cards are given an equal chance of being intermixed through the shuffling process. As we will show later, the insufficiently shuffled games of the 1980s have been defeating the same card-counting players who once handled the game in 1978 and 1979 with relative ease.

If card counters posed a threat to blackjack houses during the 1960s, New Era casino operators regained their control during the 1970s by making the conditions of play more difficult. This included increasing the number of multiple-deck games and unfavorable shuffles.

Still, card counting is an effective tool as long as you are discriminating in your selection of games. It takes a *combination* of skills, including card counting, to consistently beat the game today.

In retrospect, card counting may have been overemphasized during the 1970s. But it is still an important basic tool.

Unlike other casino games, blackjack does not have fixed odds and is not subject to the Law of Independent Trials. The Law of Independent Trials pertains to roulette, slot machines, keno, craps, the big-six wheel, or any game in which the odds have been predetermined. These odds apply to any given situation. For example, if the odds at the big-six wheel are 1 in 40 on the first spin, they will be 1 in 40 on the second spin and remain 1 in 40 through the fortieth spin. The odds never change.

In blackjack, however, the advantage continuously shifts

between the house and the players when a favorable shuffle is used. In a single-deck game, once four aces have been played, a player can calculate with absolute certainty that the odds of a blackjack are 0 percent. In other words, as cards are played, you can better determine what cards are likely yet to be played. If, in a single deck, only a few 10-value cards are played in the first half of the deck, you know that there will be many 10-value cards in the second half. If you were betting, you could raise or lower your next bet accordingly. In a game like craps, on the other hand, the odds of throwing a 7 are always 1 in 6, even if 7 has been rolled 77 times in succession.

The high-low system is an effective count for beginning players. In the high-low system, you do not count all cards. You are primarily interested in the cards most helpful to the dealer, 2 through 6, and the cards most beneficial to you—10s, face cards, and aces. The odds are in your favor, for example, when the deck is rich in 10s and aces, because you will be dealt more blackjacks and standing hands. Of course, the dealer will also be dealt more blackjacks and standing hands in this situation. But there are several major differences: the dealer must hit all stiff hands below 17 (12 through 16), meaning that he or she has a better chance of breaking, or going over 21. Also, players are paid three-to-two on blackjacks. Finally, players can double down or split their hands—they have greater options to better their hands. Dealers, on the other hand, cannot vary their play to suit their hands.

In the high-low system, cards are assigned one of three values. Cards 2 through 6 are counted as plus one ($+1$); cards 7, 8, and 9 are neutral (0), while 10s, face cards, and aces are valued at minus one (-1).

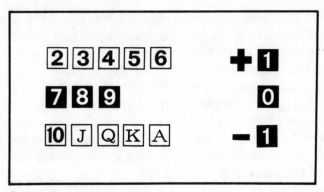

Card values of the high-low count.

A *running count* of the cards is kept as they are played. For example:

CARDS DEALT	VALUE	RUNNING COUNT
10, 10	−2	−2
5, 5, 7	+2	0
3, 10, 10, 3, 5, 4	+2	+2
J, Q, A, K, 10	−5	−3

A beginning counter can perhaps gain a slight advantage by increasing the amount of his or her bet as the count increases on the plus side. A count on the plus side means that more low cards have been played than high cards, leaving a greater number of high cards (10s, face cards, and aces) in the deck. Conversely, if the count is a minus count, −6 for example, the player will want to bet the minimum at the table, as the advantage falls more to the dealer. A more meaningful count, however, is the *true count*. The true count is calculated by dividing the running count by the number of decks yet to be played. Why is this more meaningful? Let me give you an example:

If you are playing a one-deck game and the running

count after 26 cards have been played is +6, you know that in the second half of the deck, there will be 6 more high cards than low cards. (The total value of a deck is 0; there are exactly as many high cards in a deck as low cards. If the count is positive, it means that more low cards have been played than high cards, as low cards are valued as +1 in the high-low system.) The player, in this case, has a clear advantage. If, however, the player is playing in an eight-deck game, that running count of +6 after the first 26 cards is much less meaningful. Those extra high cards remaining are distributed among 7½ remaining decks. The true count here—less than +1—is a much more meaningful evaluation of the remaining cards than the running count.

Again, the true count is calculated by dividing the running count by the number of decks (or fraction of a single deck) yet to be played. Here's how it works:

If the running count after one round in a single-deck game is +5, with three-quarters of the deck to be played, this means there are five extra high cards in the remaining 39 cards. The adjusted true count is about +7 (5 ÷ ¾ = 6.66).

With one-quarter of a deck remaining—a +5 count—there are five extra high cards in the remaining 13 cards. The adjusted true count is +20 (5 ÷ ¼) and your advantage is considerably greater than with three-quarters of a deck remaining. Let's examine an identical running count in various situations:

CARDS PLAYED	RUNNING COUNT	TRUE COUNT			
		1-Deck	2-Deck	3-Deck	4-Deck
10, Q, 5, 5, 4, K, A, 3, 4, 5, 6, A, 2.	+3	+4	+2	+1	+1

As you can see, the greater the number of decks to be played, the less the significance of the running count. Betting variations would be more dramatic in single-deck games than in multiple-deck games. For the most part, multiple-deck games are more favorable to the house than to the player.

Let's examine the meaning of a running count of +15 in multiple-deck games:

DECKS PLAYED	TRUE COUNT			
	2-Deck	4-Deck	6-Deck	8-Deck
½	+10	+4.3	+2.7	+2
1	+15	+5	+3	+2.1
2	—	+7.5	+3.8	+2.5
4	—	—	+7.5	+3.8

Basic Strategy and the Running Count

When keeping a true count, as opposed to a running count, there will be certain situations in which you should deviate from the basic-strategy rules on hitting and standing. For beginners, we have limited the number of variations to 19 that can be applied to both multiple-deck and single-deck games. We suggest you learn these 19 variations and then supplement them as you develop. Knowing these 19 variations, you can cover the hands that you will receive about 42 percent of the time, hard 12 through hard 17. These are also the hands you will most often lose. You will receive hard two-card totals of 18 or more about 24 percent of the time and two-card totals in which there are no play variations about 5 percent of the time. The following variations, then, will help you cover about 71 percent of your hands. See the illustration on page 62 for samples of flash cards that you can make:

| YOUR HAND | THE DEALER'S UP-CARD | | | | | | | | | |
	2	3	4	5	6	7	8	9	10	A
17										−7
16								+5	0	
15	−6	−7							+4	
14	−4	−5	−7							
13	−1	−2	−4	−5	−5					
12	+3	+2	0	−2	−1					

When the true count equals or is in excess of the number shown, deviate from the basic strategy. For example, with a 12 against the dealer's 2 up-card, if your true count is 3 or more, you would not hit; instead, you would stand. On either of the following two hands—12 against a dealer's 4 or 16 against a 10—you would stand on any plus count and hit on any minus count.

As for insurance, take it in multiple-deck play with a true count of three (+3) or more. In single-deck play, take insurance with a running count of two (+2) or one

| HIGH-LOW VARIATIONS | | | | | | | | | | |
	2	3	4	5	6	7	8	9	10	Æ
17										-7
16									5	O
15	-6	-7								4
14	-4	-5	-7							
13	-1	-2	-4	-5	-5					
12	3	2	O	-2	-1					

Example of homemade point count flashcards for play variations; put the dealer's up-card on upper left side, the player's hand at lower left; in the lower right, print the variation number small so it can be covered with your right thumb.

(+1) if more than 13 cards have been seen. Otherwise, do not take insurance.

In order for insurance to be worthwhile, more than one-third of the remaining unseen cards must consist of 10-value cards. In single-deck play, take insurance whenever your running count is two (+2) or more or with a running count of one (+1) if at least 13 cards have been seen and counted. In multiple-deck games, take insurance when the *true count* is two (+2) or more.

A Deck-Estimation Drill

The accuracy and effectiveness of a true count is based on your ability to estimate the number of remaining decks in the discard tray. Deck estimation must not be taken lightly. It must be done accurately and quickly.

For home drill purposes, we recommend that you purchase 24 decks of Bee brand playing cards. With 18 of the 24 decks, create the following stacks, preserving them with rubber bands:

Stack One—4 decks
Stack Two—3½ decks
Stack Three—3 decks
Stack Four—2½ decks
Stack Five—2 decks
Stack Six—1½ decks
Stack Seven—1 deck
Stack Eight—½ deck

These are your models. Learn to recognize the size of a 4-deck stack, a 3½-deck stack, and so on. Visualize them as cards remaining in the discard tray. By being able to estimate the number of cards in the discard tray, you will be able to determine the remaining decks in the shoe.

To drill, position yourself so that you cannot see the prestacked decks. Combine the remaining six decks of cards into one stack and practice cutting off cards in amounts equal to the various models. For example, cut off what you estimate to be one deck of cards and compare it with Stack Seven. We suggest you do this drill fifteen minutes a day.

Many inexperienced players have difficulty counting the single-deck game because the cards are dealt facedown. To avoid confusion and mistakes, count the cards in this manner as you see them or as they are turned over:

The dealer's up-card (your count begins).

Your own two cards.

Hits taken by each player; they will be dealt faceup.

Any player who doubles down or splits must show the two facedown cards.

The dealer's hole card and subsequent hits.

Unseen players' cards as the dealer turns them over. Do not count previously seen cards. The two original cards will always be the two nearest the dealer as the hand is exposed.

Count the cards in the same manner *every* time. Do not be tempted to count the cards of a player who inadvertently exposes his hand, because you may wind up counting the hand twice.

Counting the Game

Although cards have three classifications in the high-low system, do not use the words "plus," "minus," or "zero" while you are counting. It's a waste of brainpower and it will slow you down. When the count is minus, substitute the word "em" (M) for minus. A minus 1 becomes M1. When the count is plus, just think of the number alone. All numbers without an M are assumed to be plus. A plus 1, for example, is counted as simply 1. Use Z instead of the word "zero." This will save you time. Too often self-taught counters develop self-imposed barriers such as thinking in multi-syllabic words that hamper their speed.

Drills

In learning to count, the beginner should start with a *familiarization drill*. With a deck of cards, simply turn over one card at a time and announce the value. (Remember: +1, 0, and −1 become 1, Z, and M1.) In this drill do not add or subtract or maintain a running count. Concentrate on accuracy, not speed. Do it until you can correctly identify each card without difficulty.

After you have mastered the familiarization exercise, you should attempt the *running-count drill*. With a deck of cards, turn them over one at a time. Do not pay any attention to a card's suit or rank, just note if it is a low card $(+1)$, a high card (-1), or a neutral card (0). Before you have seen the first card, your count will be 0 (or Z).

Here's an example:

CARD SEEN	ITS VALUE	RUNNING COUNT	YOUR COUNT
Ace of spades	-1	-1	M1
Ten of hearts	-1	-2	M2
Seven of diamonds	0	-2	M2
Five of diamonds	$+1$	-1	M1
Three of spades	$+1$	0	Z
Four of hearts	$+1$	$+1$	1
Nine of hearts	0	$+1$	1

When you see a neutral card (a card with a value of 0), avoid saying "Z." Ignore the card and simply repeat the previous running count.

Many players have difficulty around the zero level, adjusting to either a plus or negative count. If this proves difficult for you, set up a deck in which there are alternating clumps of low cards and high cards. Practice until you overcome any difficulties you are having.

Stop when you have reached the fifty-first card in the deck. Since your end-of-deck count should be zero, try to determine whether the last card is high, low, or neutral before looking at it. Then turn it over and see if you are right. If you make a mistake, don't reshuffle the deck. Count the same deck again until you have corrected your error.

Another way to improve your accuracy and speed is with a *pattern-recognition drill*. In the pattern-recognition drill each two-card combination is turned over and read as a combined value. There are five possible values. This drill will prepare you to count any faceup blackjack game quickly (all Atlantic City games are dealt faceup) and will sharpen your overall effectiveness.

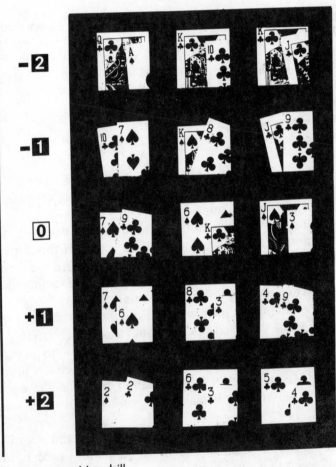

Pattern recognition drill.

In all of these drills, your priorities should be accuracy first and then speed. With regular practice, you should be able to count down a deck within forty seconds with no mistakes. Strive for twenty-five seconds with no mistakes.

To supplement your drills, make an audiocassette tape by reading off the suit and rank of each card in a deck, pausing briefly between each card. Periodically announce the running count to serve as a checkpoint later when you listen to the tape. Make two separate tapes, one at medium speed and the other somewhat faster. Play the tapes while you are driving, or on your Walkman, or at home. If you drive your car frequently during daylight hours, try counting license-plate numbers as if they were cards.

The Plus 17 Drill

An exercise that will help you perform three functions at once is called the Plus 17 Drill. For this drill, create a deck in which there are 25 low cards (2s through 6s), 8 aces, and 6 neutral cards. Deal yourself hands until you get either a soft 19 (a hand including an ace) or a hard 17. As you deal, do the following:

Total the value of each hand.

Make a hit-or-stand decision. (You may either deal an up-card for the dealer or simply recite the play for your hand against all the up-card possibilities.)

Maintain a running count.

The purpose of this drill is to give you practice counting decks in which there is an excessive number of small cards. Put each hand, intact, to one side and play through the deck. At the end of the drill, your count should be plus 17 (+17). If you have made an error, review the hands that were played.

Winning Without Counting

A noncounting method of winning at blackjack was revealed in Stanford Wong's 1978 book, *Winning Without Counting*. Designed for the Nevada game in which the dealer checks his unexposed card (the hole card) for a possible blackjack, Wong's techniques included the art of reading warped or bowed playing cards, and the science of kinesics, interpreting a dealer's body language.

Wong claimed some dealers inadvertently revealed information about the hole card after peeking at it: a twitch or a slight smile. Wong claimed remarkable success with the two techniques. Particularly warped cards. Bent previously while the dealer checked the hole card, tens and aces sometimes would develop identifiable arches. "I am right about 65 percent of the time when I think the hole card is 2 through 9." Wong wrote. He even compiled more than thirty pages of variations based on his guesswork. For players whose calculations didn't correspond with Wong's calculations, Wong provided an appendix with the appropriate variation numbers. For example, if you were right 49 percent of the time at calling 10s and aces, you could go ahead and hit a hard 17 against a dealer's 8 up-card. But you had to be able to guess correctly 64 percent of the time before you could hit a hard 17 against a 10 up-card.

If such guesswork didn't work out, Wong included other noncounting methods—better known as "cheating." One such method was to substitute the cards dealt to you with your own cards. "Be careful to match color and casino name exactly," Wong wrote. In other words, don't replace El Cortez cards with Circus Circus cards. He also advised, "I strongly recommend that you not get caught cheating." We, on the other hand, strongly recommend that you do not cheat.

According to Wong, *Winning Without Counting* is peerless. "Keep track of which specific cards are warped," Wong wrote. "At a busy table you can probably do this on paper without exciting unwelcome interest."

Wong even calculated a win rate for those accomplished in kinesics. "It is a simple matter of arithmetic," he wrote. "My guess is that expert kinesics win twice as fast as expert card counters."

There's no mathematical basis for reading warped cards or interpreting a dealer's body language. Even Wong conceded that the technique of reading warps in cards is sometimes ineffectual. "At most blackjack tables, all the cards have the same warp and thus trying to play the warps is a waste of effort or worse." In most blackjack systems there is no substitute for practice and hard work. Be suspect of any system that promises you amazing winnings and no effort. You *can* gain an edge in blackjack—but only by a careful count of the cards, by using basic strategy, and by incorporating the shuffle-tracking advice we discuss in *Break the Dealer*.

Points to Remember

1. In the high-low system, cards 2 through 6 are worth one ($+1$), cards 7, 8, and 9 are counted neutral (0), while 10s, face cards, and aces are valued at minus one (-1).

2. The true count is more meaningful than the running count. It is calculated by dividing the running count by the number of decks or fraction of the single deck to be played.

3. Do not consider playing single-deck games in which fewer than 32 cards are dealt. Make 32 the minimum—and look for 38 or more cards.

5 The Shuffle

If you want to get somewhere else, you must run at least twice as fast as that!

—LEWIS CARROLL, *Alice's Adventures in Wonderland*

In the modern game, to win consistently you must know the shuffles. It is the shuffle that has the greatest impact on the fairness of any game, whether it be single-deck or multiple-deck. Some house shuffles are more favorable for the player than others, and this chapter examines the major differences.

A random shuffle does not exist in today's casino blackjack game; it exists only in theory. What is a random shuffle? One mathematician has defined the random shuffle as equivalent to scattering the cards in a windstorm and having them retrieved by a blindfolded inebriate.

In a random shuffle, the cards in a deck or a shoe are randomly distributed. From deck to deck or shoe to shoe, there is no discernible similarity or pattern whatsoever. All blackjack strategies to date have been based upon the existence of a random shuffle—upon the fact that when cards are shuffled in a casino, they will be thoroughly intermixed. Basic strategy, as well as various card-counting systems, are dependent upon a random shuffle. In fact, however, the most you can hope for in casino play in blackjack is a degree of randomness. Richard A. Epstein, in his book *The Theory of Gambling and Statistical Logic,* states that a dealer would have to shuffle a single deck of cards up to thirty times to achieve a random shuffle. No dealer in the world has the time to shuffle each deck of cards thirty times. Houses with four-, six-, and eight-deck games would not tolerate such a time-consuming shuffling process. A random shuffle, therefore, does not exist in the practical everyday world. It is as fictional as Lewis Carroll's Alice. Yet the mathematics of blackjack are based on this nonexistent random shuffle. This means that you must be critical of various shuffling procedures used in the casinos in order to maximize your chances of benefiting from the mathematics of blackjack.

In a single-deck game, a favorable shuffle is one in which the deck is halved (approximately twenty-six cards are in each pick) and shuffled together at least three times, all cards having the opportunity to be intermixed with one another. The same concept applies to multiple-deck games. The decks are halved and picks are made from each stack, once again giving every card an opportunity to be intermixed.

An unfavorable shuffle is one in which the shuffling procedure itself restricts or interferes with the chances of each card being intermixed. A discussion of unfavorable shuffles follows.

The Unbalanced Shuffle

An unbalanced shuffle results when the dealer splits the deck irregularly before shuffling. For example, the dealer's pick A, the top portion of the deck, consists of, say, 32 cards, and pick B, the bottom portion of the deck, consists of 20 cards. The dealer makes similar unbalanced picks with each hand throughout the shuffling process and, as a result, up to 12 cards of the upper portion of pick A are not intermixed with pick B. It is possible for the top 12 cards in the deck to be preserved *throughout the shuffle.*

Blackjack dealers commonly use the unbalanced shuffle to foster excessive clumping and inhibit distribution. When new cards are introduced, because of the way card manufacturers package the cards (ace through king of one suit, king down to ace of the next), like cards tend to clump together, even after the casino "wash." This like-card clumping is very detrimental to the player, and some casinos look for shuffles that will prolong such like-card clumping as long as possible. While many dealers inadvertently make unequal picks, some dealers are required to do so because an unbalanced shuffle is the *house shuffle,* one that is dictated by management. When fresh decks of cards are put into play at houses that dictate an unbalanced shuffle, like-card or similar-card clumping is likely to persist because of the shuffling process.

The unbalanced shuffle can be exploited if the dealer is consistent with unequal picks. The end-of-deck count from the previous game would give you good information about the unplayed cards that potentially represent an identifiable clump. If the unplayed cards are placed on top of the deck prior to the shuffle and the upper portion of the deck remains the dominant pick, then you are in a position to retain or eliminate the clump with the cut card. If the clump includes an excessive number of low cards unfavorable to the player, and you are able to get the cut card, cut these cards out of play so the dealer will place them at the bottom of the deck. Of course, high cards favorable to the player would be retained.

While some dealers will readjust the size of their picks if you ask them, an occasional toke or tip for the dealer prior to the shuffle may encourage a more favorable shuffle without making you conspicuous because of your request. In houses in which dealers must follow a prescribed shuffling procedure as far as the picks are concerned, dealers will not change. Their response will be, "I'm sorry, I must follow the house shuffle." Your only recourse is to find another dealer—or another house.

The Cut Card and What It Does

The shuffle has the greatest impact on the ordering of the cards. The cut, an act of dividing the deck or decks following the shuffle, has the *second-greatest impact*. It is through knowledgeable cutting or with information gained through shuffle-tracking, which we will fully discuss in Chapter 6, that it is possible to actually have an impact on the quality of the game in which you are playing.

It should be noted here that there are two basic cutting procedures offered by the casinos. The first procedure and the most common is called the *insertion cut*, in which a player is handed a solid-color plastic card—the size of a playing card—for the purpose of dissecting the deck or decks following the shuffle. The second procedure, used only in single-deck play, is called the *lift cut*, in which the player is given the deck and is asked to physically separate the deck by lifting cards from the deck and creating a second stack. (The portion of the deck that is cut is placed behind the rest of the deck; because dealers usually only deal out three-quarters of a deck or shoe before shuffling, the bottom cards are effectively cut out of play.)

While the cut card initiates play, so to speak, it is the burn card—another solid-color plastic card that is the size of a playing card—that concludes play. It is the card that signals to the dealer the end of a deck or decks and that play must be ended at the conclusion of the round or when all of the hands currently on the table have been played out.

The Strip Shuffle

The third element having greatest impact on the ordering of the cards is called stripping. Stripping a deck sometimes precedes a shuffle. Occasionally the dealer will interrupt a shuffle to strip a deck. In a sense, stripping a deck can be likened to stripping a number of layers of wallpaper from a wall. In stripping a deck, a dealer removes cards, usually one or two at a time, from the deck and allows them to fall to the table in rapid replications. *The process simply reverses the order of the cards.* It also encourages choppy games and discourages prolonged biases. Stripping a deck has nothing to do with the shuffle; they are two separate procedures. However, when the two elements are combined, the shuffle is generally referred to as a *strip shuffle*.

The impact of stripping is more noticeable in single-deck games than in multiple-deck games because there are fewer cards. In other words, reversing the order of, say, 20 cards in a 52-card single-deck game is more dramatic than stripping 20 cards while shuffling a four-deck game, in which there are 208 cards. Some houses use the strip shuffle as a "game-control" measure when the house begins to lose. When the cards form a pattern that seems to be advantageous to the players the strip shuffle destroys that pattern. Remember, the shuffle is usually designed to maintain the general order of the cards, and is particularly effective after new playing cards are introduced. It is the strip shuffle which is often used to destroy a card clump that is advantageous to the player. Other casinos use the strip shuffle when business volume is light. Circus Circus Hotel–Casino in Las Vegas is one example of a house that uses a strip shuffle when the players begin to win.

Single-deck games in which stripping involves 10 or more cards (removed from the deck one or two cards at a time) generally should be avoided. Clump stripping (when five or more cards are stripped together in one clump) is not unfavorable to the player. When single-card stripping of 10 or more replications is casino-wide, it is a good indication that the house is not tolerant of winning players and is attempting to discourage winning before it even starts.

Two-Deck Shuffles

In many two-deck games, the decks are shuffled independently of each other. One deck is then placed on top of the other and the two halves are not intermixed. This cannot be considered a favorable shuffle and you should not be patient with any game featuring this kind of procedure, which promotes like-card clumping off new decks.

The Zone Shuffle

In shoe games (ones dealt from a shoe rather than a dealer's hand), the most common shuffle is the "zone" shuffle. In this shuffle, the cards are separated into more than two stacks—anywhere from four to eight stacks. Predetermined picks are made from the stacks. This form of shuffling inhibits distribution and often results in the rearrangement of cards in the same area of the shoe as they appeared in the previous shoe, depending on the cut.

The zone shuffle is used in the majority of shoe games on the Las Vegas Strip and in Atlantic City. Each house has a procedure for the zone shuffle that is very precise, and dealers are not allowed to deviate from it. The following is a step-by-step description of a four-deck zone shuffle that is typical of the Las Vegas Strip and Atlantic City games:

• The four-deck stack is halved, creating Stack A and Stack B.
• Stack A is halved, creating Stack C directly behind it.
• Stack B is halved, creating Stack D directly behind it.
• From the four one-deck stacks, the dealer makes half-deck cross-picks from Stack A and Stack D and then shuffles.
• Half-deck cross-picks are made from Stack C and Stack B and then shuffled.
• The procedure is completed with half-deck cross-picks and shuffles from Stack A and Stack D, followed by Stack C and Stack B. After cutting the four decks in the middle, the composition of the new shoe would look like this:

C|B
A|D
C|B
A|D

Three decks are then dealt and wind up in the discard tray. The unplayed cards are placed on top, creating this pattern:

A|D
C|B
A|D
C|B

The process is repeated for each round of play. If you simulate this procedure in your home, you will find that the zone shuffle inhibits the distribution of cards and encourages excessive like-card clumping of new cards. Through continuous shuffling, of course, the distribution will eventually improve and the game can be exploited, particularly if you utilize the shuffle-tracking techniques that are discussed in Chapter 6.

The Stutter Shuffle

The "stutter" shuffle is often used in conjunction with the zone shuffle because casinos believe it is a deterrent to shuffle-tracking teams as well as "location bettors." Although it is more difficult to track than the zone shuffle, it also can be exploited after patient scouting. Shuffle-tracking techniques examined in Chapter 6 can also be applied to the stutter shuffle.

In the stutter shuffle, the multiple-deck shoe game is divided into two stacks—Stack A and Stack B. Picks from Stack A and Stack B are shuffled, creating Stack C. Then picks from Stack A and Stack C are shuffled, followed by picks from Stack C and Stack B. Similar alternating picks are made until Stack A and Stack B are depleted.

When new decks are introduced into a shoe game, it will take at least two hours of continuous play to reduce excessive, like-card clumping. Even then, zone and stutter shuffles will prolong the clumping. The problem is distribution, or the lack of it. An exaggerated example of like-card clumping: 44444, 44444, 55555, 55555, 66666, 66666.

Imagine an eight-deck shoe in which all the 10-value cards—128 cards—were placed at the bottom. All the 9s, 8s, 7s, 6s, 5s, 4s, 3s, 2s, and aces would be together in clumps. The game would be a disaster. You would lose the majority of your double-downs and splits. Statistically, the dealer would break less than a norm of 28 percent.

The portion of the shoe dominated by the 10-value cards would be a virtual standoff. Furthermore, floor personnel would not allow you to bet in proportion to any advantage you believed that you had. Of course, this is an exaggeration. You are more likely to find clumping that is less conspicuous: 5A5, 484, 5X5, 6A6, 654, 746, 5X4, 876, 444, 4XX.

What are you looking at? Insufficiently shuffled cards. Notice the excesses and deficiencies in the 30 cards:

As: 2	3s: 0	5s: 6	7s: 2	9s: 0
2s: 0	4s: 9	6s: 5	8s: 2	Xs: 4

In this example, there is an excessive number of 4s, 5s, and 6s—"family cards"—excessive like-card clumping. In a typical multiple-deck casino game featuring either a zone or a stutter shuffle, this kind of clumping would not be dissolved within a shuffle or two.

Casinos on the Defense

In protecting their profit margins, casino operators frequently use the shuffle as a weapon to deter winning players. A typical four-step procedure when the house begins to unload, or pay off, to the players in a single-deck game is as follows:

1. Change the cards.

2. Strip-shuffle or alter the shuffle, usually utilizing unbalanced picks.

3. Speed up the game and increase the number of rounds per hour.

4. Deal fewer cards from the deck—decrease penetration—so card-counting is less effective (the fewer cards played, the less meaningful the count).

Keep in mind that many houses let a game run its course.

It's usually the smaller houses—the "grind joints" with smaller bankrolls—that are more likely to use such tactics. Of course, if an establishment is really intent about stopping you, a floor person will simply tell you to leave. When two or more of the above steps are taken by a dealer, you should consider leaving anyway. You will no longer have a favorable game.

Jerry Patterson was once told to leave a casino in downtown Las Vegas for doubling down on a soft 19 (an ace, 8) against a dealer's 6 up-card. "What do you mean?" he asked, somewhat miffed. "Sorry, your play is too strong for the house," was the reply. It was ridiculous. He had been flat-betting $100 a hand and had made a basic strategy play, at that. It was the only time in his career that he was barred for making a basic strategy play. On another occasion, Eddie Olsen was told to leave the same downtown Las Vegas casino after *flat-betting* two hands for several rounds. Eddie told the floor person he was down by $150. "And that's the way we're going to keep it," the floor person replied.

In multiple-deck games, it is the shuffle itself that is the major deterrent to the skilled player today, and a number of onetime computer consulting firms are actually specializing in *shuffle analysis and design*. In fact, one major West Coast university has also entered the field and its efforts were displayed at a Las Vegas Strip casino beginning in early 1986.

"Shuffles are generally changed to improve the hold [or blackjack win rate]," one assistant casino manager told us. "Sometimes a shuffle is changed because the hold is too high . . . and driving away business [because the players are unable to win]." In general, most casino managers refused to discuss their table holds or blackjack win rates or *how and why* a new shuffling procedure is developed.

While documenting twenty-eight major modifications to shuffles used in Atlantic City casinos between 1982 and 1985, we monitored nine casinos in both New Jersey and Nevada continuously. The monitored casinos used multiple-deck shoe games with either a zone or stutter shuffle. Overall, we detected a 3 percent improvement in the win rate among players three hours after the introduction of new cards on 391 dates and an 8-percent improvement after six hours. At the same time, dealer-breaking activity increased from 21 percent to 26 percent (about normal) during the same period.

A Winner's Guideline

If you follow this simple guideline, you don't need to be an *expert* on shuffles to evaluate the game of any house:

• Watch several dealers shuffle. If it is a single-deck game, are the dealers stripping the deck or using unbalanced picks when they shuffle the cards? If the answer is yes, don't bother with the game; go someplace else.

• For multiple-deck games, do the dealers use a zone shuffle or a stutter shuffle? If they do, proceed with caution. In Chapter 6, we'll give you some additional tips for these particular games.

• While standing or sitting at a blackjack table, pay attention to the dealer's shuffle between games. If it has been a winning table, watch for any alteration in the dealer's shuffle; any change in the shuffle is strong evidence that the dealer or the house may be making an attempt to break up the game with legitimite "game-control" methods. If the game suddenly goes bad, do not hesitate to leave.

• Never sit down at a table for the first two hours of

play after new cards have been introduced. It is almost impossible to win.

Finally, here's a playing tip.

When you're in a game, be friendly and outgoing with the dealer, the floor personnel, and the other players. Don't forget to occasionally tip the dealer at the top of the shuffle, particularly when you're in Las Vegas, Laughlin, or Reno. We are convinced that this practice has resulted in additional winnings for both of us by prolonging favorable games because the dealer also had "a piece of the action" and is not likely to voluntarily alter the shuffle—or, the game—while being toked. Besides, it's good cover; card counters have a reputation for not toking. So the New Era player does just the opposite.

6 Shuffle-Tracking

A deck of cards was built like the purest of hierarchies, with every card a master to those below it, a lackey to those above it.

—ELY CULBERTSON

"Shuffle-tracking" is the science of following specific cards through the shuffling process for the purpose of either keeping them in play or cutting them out of play. It is not an alternative to card counting; it is used in conjunction with card counting.

Tracking is a powerful tool. It can be used to perpetuate a favorable game as well as to *create* a favorable game. When you are capable of influencing a game in this manner, you are playing blackjack at its highest level.

Tracking cards is not new, although relatively little has been published on the subject. A group of low-profile players effectively used shuffle-tracking techniques in Atlantic City between 1979 and 1981. Jerry Patterson formed his first tracking team in 1982 and the earliest results were not impressive. The methods looked good on paper but needed to be modified for the realities of casino play. Eddie Olsen has also worked with a number of experimental mini-teams through the years, refining and simplifying crude and complicated methods. We have both concluded that tracking is best suited for partner or mini-team play, although a handful of players have incorporated effective tracking techniques into their individual play. These individuals have been successful because they developed ways of accurately maintaining and plotting a number of "side counts" or tabulations that are in addition to a card counter's regular count.

In multiple-deck play, keeping side counts of, say, all the aces, 5s, and 7s that you have seen played is not sufficient. You must also be able to identify areas of the shoe that may be rich or poor in aces, 5s, and 7s. You must also be able to predict what kind of impact the shuffling process will have on any clumps that you may detect. With this kind of information, however, you can have a dramatic impact on the game when the dealer hands you or a confederate the cut card. With the cut card, you can make a decision about which cards you want to keep in play.

Tracking is for the dedicated, advanced player who is seeking an additional, though admittedly undetermined, advantage over the house. There are various methods to track any shuffle. This chapter will examine *basic* tracking methods that can be used in individual play as well as methods suitable for partner and team play.

In tracking, you apply your running count as you would normally, using it as a guide for making play variations and in insurance decisions. In tracking, you use your running count additionally to determine the value of the unplayed or unseen cards. For example, in an eight-deck game in which two decks are cut from play, an end-of-shoe count of, say, minus five would tell you that there are five extra small cards, or cards valued 2 through 6, in the unplayed or unseen cards.

In addition, during the course of the game, you should have already accumulated per-deck distribution of certain key cards such as all aces, 5s, and 10-value cards that have been played. This is done with side counts, which are nothing more than additional counts. In addition to aces, 5s, and 10-value cards, some players keep track of additional cards, such as 7s or 8s, key neutral, or 0-value, cards. The more side counts you are capable of maintaining, the more information you will have accumulated to accurately "profile" a multiple-deck shoe.

Storing or keeping track of this information is the biggest problem. No, you don't need a personal computer at the blackjack table. But you do need aids, and casino chips can be used as an abacus for side counts. They can also be used to designate per-deck values and as aids in simulating multiple-deck shuffles, as you will learn.

Chips can be arranged on the table in the various positions of a clock face. For example, a red chip with the casino logo or denomination turned to one o'clock could represent plus 1; a green chip turned to one o'clock could indicate minus 1. In this way, a chip could hold the count up to a plus or minus 12. If the casino chips have two distinct sides, "heads and tails" so to speak, then you could store an additional plus or minus 12 worth of information—or up to plus 24 and minus 24—with the chips. You will need to improvise according to the conditions.

In per-deck tracking, you are keeping score on excesses and deficiencies. Chips then can represent whole decks and can be staggered to the left or right to designate plus or minus counts. For example, the third chip of a stack staggered to the left could mark a surplus of 10-value cards and aces in the third deck; the fourth chip staggered to the right, a deficiency in the fourth deck; and so on.

It would be worthwhile for the high-low counter to track minus decks or decks with an excess of high cards in multiple-deck games. This could be done with just two colors of casino chips of different denominations: a base color and an off-color to identify high-card clumps. This would require keeping an eye on the discard tray to estimate the number of cards played and making a count adjustment at the end of each deck to determine the previous deck's worth.

At the end of the shoe, use your end-of-shoe count to determine the value of the unplayed cards, profiling the decks with chips. An eight-deck shoe would be represented by eight chips—one chip per deck. If the house uses a straightaway shuffle, one is which the shoe is halved and picks are then shuffled from each half, it is possible to track the clumps by simply intermixing your chips. This should put you within one deck of accuracy, which is sufficient for cutting purposes. Your precision will not be strong enough to bet on, but it should keep the cards that are favorable in play and increase your chances of winning on subsequent shoes.

You won't always have strong information in order to intelligently cut the cards. But when you do, you must try to gain the cut card if it has been given to someone else. The best way to get it? Ask for it. "Do you mind if I cut?" and "I feel lucky, let me cut this shoe" are two approaches that usually work. Many players believe the cut is an insignificant ritual. If you are unable to gain the cut card, your information is still useful. You may be able to calculate if you will be staying in the game or leaving, based on the quality of someone else's cut.

In team or partner play, the first objective in shuffle-tracking is to profile a shoe or play a shoe in order to analyze the distribution of selected cards. You should have predetermined objectives such as keeping the 10-value cards and aces in play or creating a game in which there is excessive dealer-breaking activity. In the latter case, your objectives would then be to create a shortage of aces, a key middle-range card such as a 4, 5, or 6, and a neutral-value card such as a 7 or 8. At the same time, you would attempt to promote normal distribution of 10-value cards.

The example that follows is for mini-team use. Table assignments are made for each member of the team. In this case, the assignments include a count of 10-value cards as well as use of the high-low counting system. The game to be tracked is six decks with one deck cut out of play.

There are 16 ten-value cards in one deck and 96 in a six-deck game. We will use a 50-percent ratio to evaluate each deck. A 50-percent excess for one deck, therefore, is defined as 24 or more 10-value cards. This is 16 plus 50 percent of 16, or 24. A deficiency for one deck is defined as 8 or fewer. Normal distribution could be defined as between 9 and 23 10-value cards. Here are the conditions and objectives for our mini-team example:

- Shuffle to be tracked: A favorable shuffle.
- Tracking tools: Multiple-colored casino chips; each chip equal to one deck of cards. Chips are effective because they will not stand out. Some players who track use specially designed jewelry such as cigarette lighters with dials that can be conspicuous.
- Tracking code: Each deck will be represented by a single chip. One white casino chip will signify 50-percent deficiency of 10-value cards (8 or fewer); one green casino chip will signify 50-percent excess (24 or more); one red casino chip will signify normal distribution (9–23).
- Minimum number of players required: Two (one "profiler" and one "counter").

• First objective: To profile excesses and deficiencies of 10-value cards in a six-deck game.

• Second objective: To maintain the majority of 10-value cards throughout subsequent shoes.

The game begins:

Deck 1: Twenty-five 10-value cards are played. The "profiler" designates the deck with one green chip, signaling an excess of high cards.

Deck 2: Seven 10-value cards are played. One white chip is placed on top of the green chip, signaling that Deck 2 contains a deficiency of high cards.

Deck 3: Eight 10-value cards are played. One white chip is added to the white and green chips.

Deck 4: Twenty-four 10-value cards are played. One green chip is added to the stack.

Deck 5: Sixteen 10-value cards are played. The stack is topped by one red chip.

At this point, the dealer is ready to place the sixth, unplayed deck on top of the five decks that have been played, halve the shoe, and shuffle. The "profiler," meanwhile, has counted 80 ten-value cards played, leaving 16 in the unplayed deck. One more red chip is added to the stack to signify the last deck and the six-deck game has been profiled.

The dealer, having put the sixth deck on top of the five decks that have been played and dividing the shoe in half or two equal stacks, now shuffles, taking one-deck picks from each stack. The shuffle results in a marriage of decks 6|3, 5|2, and 4|1. The "profiler" arranges the chips accordingly. The margin of error with this technique is one deck, too great for betting purposes, but sufficient for cutting purposes.

In this example, 49 of the 96 10-value cards are now

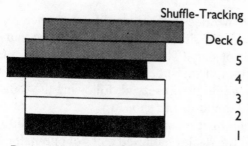

Shuffle-Tracking

Deck 6
5
4
3
2
1

Decks of cards represented by casino chips.

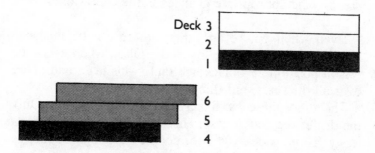

Deck 3
2
1

6
5
4

Decks of cards represented by casino chips as the dealer prepares to shuffle.

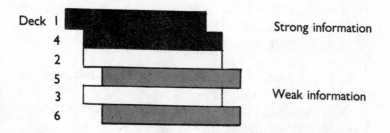

Deck 1   Strong information
4
2
5
3   Weak information
6

Decks of cards represented by casino chips after the dealer has shuffled.

within the first two decks. You would not chance a thin cut off the top in this situation because you might cut 10-value cards out of play. The correct cut would be a thin cut off the bottom of the shoe. This way, the cards in the first two decks would be preserved, following the thin cut of cards from the end of the shoe.

Tracking techniques must be adjusted to the conditions. For example, if the dealer had used picks of one-half deck for the shuffle, the mini-team would have to compensate by tracking in half-decks, using twelve chips instead of six, making appropriate changes in the code values.

Even when you're an expert, there can be mishaps. There was one instance for Eddie Olsen when everyone was in position at a blackjack table—his team had taken over all the seats, but things did not go well.

The atmosphere was like a cemetery at the casino. Only the dealer seemed at ease. He shuffled calmly and effortlessly. Three wide-eyed floor people stared in disbelief as all seven players appeared to be building castles with their multiple-colored chips. All the players, that is, except one.

Roy couldn't separate his chips. The suction of the metallic one-dollar coins had locked them into his red chips.

"I don't believe this," he said.

The dealer was almost finished shuffling.

"Shuffle your chips, Roy, shuffle them," Eddie whispered.

Roy had tracked the aces, but couldn't simulate the dealer's shuffle with his chips.

Then, another player, Sandy, knocked over his chips, one of them rolling into the dealer's tray.

The dealer retrieved the chip and smiled.

"This reminds me of a Marx Brothers movie," Sandy said.

The tracking team eventually overcame its shaky start

and the players' chips multiplied; the dealer broke in excess of 38 percent. The floor personnel weren't particularly pleased with the proceedings. They finally changed the cards, but not before Eddie's team had won a good deal of money.

Don't be obvious about the fact that you are shuffle-tracking. If the dealer's shuffle never varies and is predictable, adjust or shuffle your chips before the cards are shuffled. Handle your chips as if you are playing with them. This is not unusual; many players fumble or fidget with their chips.

The dollar value of tracking is intangible. It can be the difference between a $200 win and a $400 win because of one accurate cut. The one potential drawback is the beginner's temptation to attempt surgery by manipulating the cut on a game that isn't there; this can be expensive. When starting out, your objective should be to improve or prolong a proven game, not create one. Only when you are accomplished and operating in a team situation with a number of others should you consider creating a favorable game from scratch.

The most significant reason for this is that there are limitations on what one player can do swiftly and accurately. In team or partner play, the side counts can be divided among several individuals. Ideally, one player should make the cutting decision based on the information that is available on the table in the form of the players' chips. That decision can then be relayed to the person who has the cut card, either through hand signals or through the placement of chips.

Mathematical Tracking

An ideal team tracking method for the zone shuffle is to actually calculate half-deck or three-quarter-deck values, depending on the number of decks cut out of play and the size of the dealer's picks.

In the example that follows, we will simulate another six-deck game with one deck cut out of play. Other conditions and objectives:

- Shuffle to be tracked: The zone shuffle.
- Tracking tools: Casino chips (clock method) and the high-low counting system.
- Number of players required: Seven.
- Job assignments: Four "clockers" keep half-deck counts of the marriage of the following half-decks: 3|9, 4|10, 5|7, and 6|8. A fifth clocker will use the end-of-shoe count in an effort to make a determination about the merger of half-decks 1|11 and 2|12. A sixth player will signal the high-low count to others, if necessary, for playing decisions. A seventh player, the analyzer, will cut the game, based on all available information.
- First objective: To profile a minimum of eight half-decks, twelve if possible, for the purpose of maintaining the strongest possible game.
- Second objective: To maintain as many favorable cards as possible within half-decks 3 through 10 and to relocate unfavorable cards to half-decks 1-2 and 11-12.

The precision of the zone shuffle makes it relatively easy to track, but you must correlate your tracking unit to the size of the dealer's picks.

In the most common procedure, the dealer would divide the six decks into two three-deck stacks with decks 1, 2, and 3 on the left (becoming half-decks 1–6) and decks 4, 5, and 6 on the right (becoming half-decks 7–12). Each three-deck stack is then made into three one-deck stacks, creating a total of six stacks.

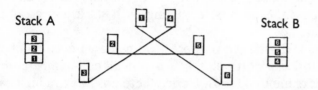

Stack A

Stack B

At the beginning of this zone shuffle, six 1-deck stacks are created from two 3-deck stacks (A and B). The connecting lines indicate the half-deck zones to be shuffled.

Deck no.	value	½ deck no.
6	+▦	12
	-▦	11
5	+▦	10
	-▦	9
4	+▦	8
	-▦	7
3	+▦	6
	-▦	5
2	+▦	4
	-▦	3
1	+▦	2
	-▦	1

merged half-decks	total value
①+⑪	-▨
③+⑨	-▨
⑤+⑦	·▨
②+⑫	+▨
④+⑩	+▨
⑥+⑧	+▨

Taking half-deck picks, the dealer would draw from stacks 3 and 4, 2 and 5, 1 and 6—in that order—and then repeat the process, depleting each stack and creating a new shoe.

For illustrative purposes, we made all even-numbered half-decks worth plus 4 ($+4$) and all odd-numbered half-decks minus 4 (-4). Notice there are 24 extra high cards within three decks and 24 extra low cards within three decks.

Deck 6 before the shuffle represents unseen or unplayed cards. When its half-decks (11 and 12) are merged with half-decks 1 and 2, you will have insufficient information to profile decks 6 and 3 of each new shoe.

End-of-Shoe Tracking

A simple method for tracking the straightaway shuffle (one in which the deck or decks are divided equally and picks of about the same size are made from each stack and shuffled together) that can be done by one player involves using the end-of-shoe count to determine the value of the unplayed cards and combining it with the deck it will marry during the shuffle.

Let's take a six-deck game with one deck cut out of play as an example. Decks 1 through 5 represent the cards that have been played. Deck 6 represents the unplayed cards. The dealer moves deck 6 to the top of deck 5 and prepares to shuffle. Your end-of-shoe count, meanwhile, was plus 8 ($+8$), which means the value of the unplayed cards is minus 8 (-8) and includes eight extra high cards.

The dealer divides the shoe into two stacks for the shuffle, putting decks 6, 5, and 4 on one side and decks 3, 2, and 1 on the other. Deck 6 will marry deck 3. If you had calculated the count for deck 3 as it was played and knew its value was, for example, minus 8 (-8), you would know the values of decks 6 and 3 combined was minus 16 (-16)—that it had 16 extra high cards. You would cut these two decks into play for the new shoe. Conversely, if the value of the two decks was plus 16 ($+16$), you would cut them out of play, realizing there would be 16 extra high cards in the four other decks.

Our most accurate tracking team included the two of us, an attorney with the city of Philadelphia, an official from the state of New York—and Alice, a fifty-two-year-old grandmother from Pennsylvania.

Despite our Model T tracking techniques—this was one of our earliest teams—the players made few mistakes, performed like professionals, and had a sense of humor. Our favorite target was a casino in Atlantic City that used a double stutter shuffle in an eight-deck game that was relatively easy to track.

Our objective at this particular casino was to create a shortage of aces, 5s, and 7s, resulting in excessive dealer-breaking activity. One of us would track excesses and deficiencies of the cards while three other players would profile the unplayed cards. Information was passed with hand signals and it usually took three shoes to "set up" a game, depending on distribution problems. When the "big shoe" was due, Olsen would whisper to one of the players, "This is it." The player would then pass the word to the others.

Over a five-month experimental period, we had a good win rate in table takeovers (nearly 70 percent) and the risk or investment factor was relatively low. Surprisingly, the biggest problem was sustaining a favorable game, a challenge Eddie finally solved with his eighth tracking team. In many of the games, the team achieved dealer-breaking activity in excess of 35 percent. The norm for the team was 30 percent and the two best games were nearly 50 percent. Normally the dealer breaks about 28 percent of the time. The more often the dealer breaks, the more often the players win.

Sometimes, even after a team has worked hard to set up a game, all its effort is for naught. Such was the case with us one April night. It had been a tough game. After four shoes, Eddie finally whispered to a teammate, "This is it." The teammate passed the word and the players watched the dealer shuffle with great expectations. But as the dealer removed the cards from the table to put them into the shoe, she dropped the cards.

The players stared at the strewn cards in total silence. It was as if they had just witnessed a plane crash. One player stumbled from his chair. Another player stormed from the table, swinging his arms like a pendulum, and shouted, "I don't believe it!" One player started to laugh. Soon all the players were laughing. What else could we do? Four shoes of work was now like spilled milk. Did the dealer do it intentionally? Probably not, but we'll never know for sure. The team left the table.

Tracking Hand-Held Games

Eddie Olsen has made significant breakthroughs in shuffle-tracking, primarily in the study of card movement and what he describes as "gap tracking." Because gap tracking is unique to his play, he has declined to discuss more advanced shuffle-tracking techniques here. However, tracking hand-held games in Nevada, particularly two-deck games, can be done in much the same manner as we have described for multiple-deck games.

Since penetration—or the number of cards dealt or put into play—is only one deck for the majority of two-deck games in Nevada, we suggest that beginning shuffle-trackers track half-decks, or 26-card sections, using four casino chips for the purpose of profiling the decks. After you have gained some tracking experience, you may then want to convert to quarter-deck tracking (plotting 13-card sections), using eight casino chips instead of four. While the method may seen cumbersome, it is well worth the additional effort. As is the case with shoe games, you should not base your betting on tracking. The purpose, again, is to perpetuate or improve a game based on intelligent cutting of the decks.

Home-Study Suggestions

1. Simulate in full a particular casino game, the one you intend to play, no matter if it's an eight-deck game at Resorts International Casino–Hotel in Atlantic City or a six-deck game from the Dunes Hotel and Casino in Las Vegas. Simulate the shuffle *exactly*.

2. Select the most appropriate method from this chapter for tracking the game you have selected (chips, hand signals, clock positions of chip faces, etc.).

3. Don't practice with coins or poker chips. Use the real thing, casino chips. Also practice with Bee brand or casino playing cards.

4. Practice reading the discard tray until you are able to accurately estimate it within one-eighth of a deck for 1 to 3 decks and one-quarter of a deck for 4 to 6 decks. Utilize the Deck Estimation Drill described in Chapter 4, if necessary.

5. Create seven-player games, tracking 10-value cards and aces. Mark per-deck excesses of 40 percent or more with an off-colored chip. Do not mark normal or deficient decks for this drill.

6. After the cards have been played and shuffled, simulate the exact shuffle with your chips, remembering that your objective is to be accurate within two decks.

7. After the chips have been shuffled, determine the best cut possible to keep any excessive 10-value cards and aces in play. Cut the shoe and then analyze your effort, scanning the cards. Did you succeed in keeping them in play? Remember, you will not be using this procedure for betting purposes.

8. Through repetition, you will become more at ease handling the chips. Inside the casino, you must move the chips quickly and smoothly without attracting attention.

9. After you have become proficient at tracking excesses, try following deficiencies as well. This will require using three colors of chips. One color to designate neutral, one to designate excess, and one to designate deficiency. Follow Step 7 in grading your accuracy.

10. After you have developed your skills and are reasonably confident, look for a low-stakes game and test yourself under actual casino conditions. But first, *become proficient at home.*

7 Money Management

*Money means nothing. If you really cared about it, you wouldn't
be able to sit down at a poker table and bluff off fifty thousand
dollars.*

—CHIP REESE (POKER PLAYER), *The Biggest Game in Town*

Our money-management recommendations may seem
unorthodox, but they work. They are based on a tough,
street-style approach to blackjack. An approach that shows
great respect for the game.

We stress focusing on each hand and each bet. Do you
have the correct amount down? If it's time to bet five
units, put five units on the line—not four or six. Do not
focus on the possible outcome. Play the game just as dis-
passionately as if it were chess. You must regard chips as
if they were only game pieces, to be bet according to
specific rules.

In this chapter, we will outline various money-management methods such as betting with "The Kelly Criterion,"
the true count, and the running count. These are all traditional methods. We will also outline our own money-
management program that we believe effectively deals
with the modern game.

Creating Your Bankroll

Your "bankroll" is all the money you decide to put aside
for blackjack, whether it's $300 or $3,000. It does not

include money you will need to cover your expenses, such as hotel charges, meals, etc. Nor does it include cash due or expected. It must not include money available through credit cards or casino credit. Your bankroll is only the cash you have on hand.

Once you've decided how much money to include in your casino bankroll, break it down in the following manner:

1. The total casino bankroll. This is all the money you decide to put aside for blackjack play, whether it's $3,000 or $300.

2. Your trip bankroll. Your trip bankroll is the amount of money you take with you on any one trip to the casinos. It should equal one-half or your total casino bankroll.

3. Your session bankroll. Your session bankroll is equal to one-fifth of your trip bankroll. This will also serve as your automatic *stop-loss*. In other words, if you lose one-fifth of your trip bankroll in any one session, this is when you stop for that session.

A *session* is defined as one day or night of play, continuous or not. A session could be one hour or twelve hours, depending on your objectives and stamina. On a one-night trip to Atlantic City, your trip bankroll and session bankroll are the same. On a two-night stay in Atlantic City, it is likely that your trip would comprise two sessions.

The amount of your bankroll determines the amount of your maximum bet as well as the spread between your minimum and maximum bet, and your stop-loss—the amount at which, if you lose, you stop for the evening. Here is how to determine these amounts based on your bankroll:

Maximum Bet: The highest bet you will make. Your maximum bet should be equal to one-fiftieth of your casino bankroll, or one twenty-fifth of your current trip bankroll. For example, if your casino bankroll is $1,000, your maximum bet will be $20. If your casino bankroll is $2,500, your maximum bet is $50.

Minimum Bet: The lowest bet you will make is equal to one-hundredth of your casino bankroll. If your bankroll is $1,000, your minimum bet will be $10. If your bankroll is $2,500, your minimum bet is $25.

Your minimum bet should be based on the mathematics of your bankroll—not on the minimums of tables that are open. For example, if your minimum bet should be $3, based on your bankroll, and the only tables available have minimums of $5, $10, and $15, you *should not play*. Atlantic City casinos encourage people to overbet during crowded periods with an excessive number of $10 and $15 table minimums. Statistically, Atlantic City casinos have calculated that the average visitor has a bankroll of $300, which is not sufficient to play a $10 table.

Betting Spread: This number is the ratio of your minimum bet to your maximum bet. If your maximum bet is $20 and your minimum bet is $10, your betting spread is 2 to 1.

Stop-Loss: The maximum amount you will risk losing during one casino session is equal to one session bankroll. A *stop-loss* is the total amount that you can lose in a session, whether it is a one-hour session or a twelve-hour session. Here are some examples:

CASINO BANKROLL	TRIP BANKROLL	SESSION BANKROLL	*MINIMUM BET	MAXIMUM BET	STOP-LOSS
$ 500	$ 250	$ 50	$2–3	$ 10	$ 50
750	375	75	3–5	15	75
1,000	500	100	5	20	100

*Calculated lower than actual minimums, where the table minimums are $5 or higher.

CASINO BANKROLL	TRIP BANKROLL	SESSION BANKROLL	*MINIMUM BET	MAXIMUM BET	STOP-LOSS
$ 1,500	$ 750	$ 150	$ 5	$ 30	$ 150
2,000	1,000	200	5	40	200
2,500	1,250	250	5	50	250
5,000	2,500	500	10	100	500
10,000	5,000	1,000	25	200	1,000

*Calculated lower than actual minimums, where the table minimums are $5 or higher.

One of the most important considerations in your money-management strategy is the difference between your minimum bet and your maximum bet. This is called the *spread*. The idea is that you will lose the majority of your minimum bets, and win the majority of your maximum bets. In fact, you are likely to lose more bets overall than you win. But you can win money, even if you do lose the majority of your bets. How? If you lose four $10 bets, but win the fifth bet of $50, you'll end up winning $10. This is why the spread is important.

Most of the players on the East Coast don't stand much of a chance of finding tables with minimums of $2, $3, or $5 during primetime periods. The majority of the blackjack tables have minimums of $10, $15, and $25. Ben A. Borowsky, former spokesman of the New Jersey Casino Control Commission and now publisher of the *Casino Chronicle,* says blackjack players in the East are accustomed to being "overcharged." New Era casino operators know the average Saturday-night gambler has a bankroll of $300. With these kinds of table minimums, it isn't likely that many of these players will walk away winners—it takes relatively few bad hands to drive them into bankruptcy—"ruin." Casinos are not undercapitalized. Most gamblers *are* either undercapitalized or do not bet in proportion to their bankroll. If your bankroll cannot accommodate $10, $15, and $25 table minimums, you must not play. Do not allow any casino to force you to overbet. You simply cannot win this way.

The Kelly Criterion

One of the most interesting and sensible betting systems is the J. L. Kelly Criterion. In this system, you bet your advantage in proportion to your current resources. A significant drawback of this system is that it requires continuous calculations at the blackjack table. Your risk of ruin, however, is 0 percent. Theoretically, it is not possible for you to lose all your money when you are using this system.

How does it work? Let's say you have a $5,000 bankroll. If, on a given hand, you had a 3-percent advantage, you could bet 3 percent, or $150, of your bankroll. If you won the hand, you would recalcuate your bankroll at $5,150. If, on the other hand, you had lost the hand, your new bankroll would be $4,850. Subsequent bets would be based on your current bankroll and your advantage. (Note: A player's advantage is never calculated on the basis of the running count, but is more closely approximated by calculating the true count. Even then, your advantage may be only about 50 percent of your true count, based upon the house rules and the number of decks.) Here's a series of examples with the bets rounded down:

HAND	BANKROLL	ADVANTAGE	APPROXIMATE BET	RESULT
1	$5,000	3%	$150	Won
2	5,150	4%	200	Won
3	5,350	2%	100	Lost
4	5,250	1%	50	Lost
5	5,200	3%	150	Won
6	5,350	0	5	Push

Obviously, such a betting spread is unrealistic. The casinos would immediately recognize you as a card counter and constantly "shuffle up" on you whenever the count began to go in your favor. About the highest bet spread you can hope to get away with is a spread of 3 to 1. The problem is that in neutral or negative decks, the recommended bet size is 1/1000 of your bankroll in order for the Kelly system to work properly. Still, the Kelly Criterion can be an effective money-management tool in positive decks.

The house rules and number of decks being played are significant factors in determining your real advantage in any game under the Kelly system. As your true count increases, your advantage increases. In the Las Vegas single-deck game, your advantage begins when you achieve a true count of one ($+1$). Percentage-wise, your advantage is approximately 50 percent of your true count ($+5 = 2\frac{1}{2}\%$), but this number will vary slightly based on the house rules and the number of decks used.

True-Count Betting

When you find a game with a favorable shuffle and there is a correlation between what is happening in the game and your true count, you should bet with the true count.

What do we mean by a correlation between the true count and what is actually happening at the table? Are players drawing 10-value cards in double-down situations with a strong plus count? Is the dealer breaking when showing a low card with a high plus count most of the time? If so, then there seems to be a correlation between the count and the cards that come up. If the dealer, on the other hand, is frequently making hands on multiple-card draws in big plus-count situations, there is *not* a correlation between the true count and what is actually happening in the game. We often refer to this correlation as integrity. If the game has integrity, then the cards you would expect to come up, in a high or a low true-count situation, tend to in fact be drawn.

Your risk of ruin for an eight-hour session is less than one percent if you bet with the true count and vary your maximum bet according to your current bankroll (a method adapted from the Kelly Criterion). When you calculate the true count (the running count divided by the number of decks or the fraction of the deck to be played), always round *down;* this also holds true for making play variations.

The true-count betting schedule in this chapter may be used after calculating your true count in this manner:

1. Determine the running count.

2. Estimate the number of decks or fraction of the deck in the discard tray.

3. Subtract your estimate from the total number of decks being dealt in the game.

4. To compute the true count, divide the running count by the number of decks remaining. Then, if you choose, subtract one, for the purpose of "rounding down," or compensating for any errors that you have made.

In the true-count betting table, we have listed bankroll sizes, betting spreads, and the dollar amount per true count. The "Dollars Per True Count" is another way of determining your betting unit based on your bankroll. For example, with a $234 bankroll, you would be betting $1 per true count. In a true-count situation of +5, your bet would be $5. With a $1,173 bankroll, however, you would bet $5 per true count. In the same +5 true-count situation, your bet would be $25. In still another example, if your bankroll was in the $4,692 range, you would be betting $20 per true count. In a +5 situation, your bet would be $100.

We have listed a stop-loss that should be considered

mandatory. The following table is for six or more decks only:

DOLLARS PER TRUE COUNT	BANKROLL	SPREAD	MAXIMUM BET	STOP-LOSS
$ 1	$ 234	$ 2–5	$ 5	$ 40
2	469	2–10	10	80
3	704	2–15	15	120
4	938	2–20	20	160
5	1,173	2–25	25	200
6	1,408	2–30	30	240
7	1,642	5–35	35	280
8	1,877	5–40	40	320
9	2,111	5–45	45	360
10	2,346	5–50	50	400
11	2,581	5–55	55	440
12	2,815	5–60	60	480
13	3,050	5–65	65	520
14	3,284	5–70	70	560
15	3,519	5–75	75	600
16	3,754	5–80	80	640
17	3,988	10–85	85	680
18	4,222	10–90	90	720
19	4,457	10–95	95	760
20	4,692	10–100	100	800

We do not recommend a "stop-win." However, we suggest that when you win an amount equal to your stop-loss figure, you lock up 80 percent of your profit. For example, with a $3,050 bankroll, once you have won $520 (the stop-loss number), lock up $416 of the win and play with the remaining $104. This way, you will leave the game with at least a $416 profit, even if you succumb to a run of bad luck.

*   *   *

There is another method of computing the true count that you may find more efficient. Instead of dividing the running count by the remaining number of decks, multiply by the inverse of remaining decks. This will require memorizing the multipliers listed below. For example, if in an eight-deck game there are 5.5 decks remaining with a running count of 14, instead of dividing by 5.5, you would use the multiplier of .2 from the table to compute the true count of 2.8. For four-deck games, use the multipliers listed between 3.5 decks and one deck.

The true-count multipliers:

MULTIPLE-DECK GAMES

Remaining Decks	Multiplier	Remaining Decks	Multiplier
7.5	0.15	4.0	0.25
7.0	0.15	3.5	0.3
6.5	0.15	3.0	0.3
6.0	0.15	2.5	0.4
5.5	0.2	2.0	0.5
5.0	0.2	1.5	0.7
4.5	0.2	1.0	1.0

SINGLE-DECK GAMES

Cards Played	Multiplier	Cards Played	Multiplier
13	1.3	26	2.0
17	1.5	33	3.0
		39	4.0

Running-Count Betting

If you do not intend to incorporate the true count into your play, your running count still can be an effective tool in betting. Remember that the running count is much more significant in multiple-deck play after 50 percent of the cards have been played. Mentally divide the discard tray into three zones and calculate the appropriate bet based on the running-count betting schedules in this chapter. We have defined zones for four-deck, six-deck, and eight-deck games, calculating corresponding schedules based on bankrolls.

Running-Count Zones (Four-Deck Game)
The Discard Tray

		Do not raise your bet until the count equals:
2²/₃ decks or more in the discard tray	Zone 3	+1
1¹/₃ to 2²/₃ decks	Zone 2	+2
0 to 1¹/₃ decks	Zone 1	+4

Running-Count Zones (Six-Deck Game)
The Discard Tray

		Do not raise your bet until the count equals:
4 decks or more in the discard tray	Zone 3	+2
2 to 4 decks	Zone 2	+3
0 to 2 decks	Zone 1	+5

Running-Count Zones (Eight-Deck Game)
The Discard Tray

		Do not raise your bet until the count equals:
6 decks or more in the discard tray	Zone 4	+1
4 to 6 decks	Zone 3	+3
2 to 4 decks	Zone 2	+5
0 to 2 decks	Zone 1	+7

RUNNING-COUNT BETTING SCHEDULES FOR FOUR-DECK GAMES

The numbers represent the dollars to be bet per running count.

Casino Bankroll	Zone 1 +4 or more	Zone 2 +2 or more	Zone 3 +1 or more
$ 1,000	$1	$ 2	$ 4
1,500	2	3	6
2,000	2.50	4	8
3,000	4	6	12
4,000	5	8	16
5,000	6	10	20
6,000	7	12	24
7,000	9	14	28
8,000	10	16	32
9,000	11	18	36
10,000	12	20	40

FOR SIX-DECK GAMES

The numbers represent the dollars to be bet per running count.

Casino Bankroll	Zone 1 +5 or more	Zone 2 +3 or more	Zone 3 +2 or more
$ 1,000	$0.50	$ 1.50	$ 2
1,500	1	2	2.50
2,000	1.50	3	4
3,000	2	4	6
4,000	2	5	8
5,000	3	6	10
6,000	4	7	12
7,000	4	10	14
8,000	5	11	16
9,000	5	12	18
10,000	6	13	20

FOR EIGHT-DECK GAMES

The numbers represent the dollars to be bet per running count.

Casino Bankroll	Zone 1 +7 or more	Zone 2 +5 or more	Zone 3 +3 or more	Zone 4 +1 or more
$ 1,000 ...	$0.50	$1	$ 1.50	$ 2.50
1,500 ...	1	1.50	2	3
2,000 ...	1	1.50	2.50	5
3,000 ...	2	2.50	4	7
4,000 ...	2	3	5	10
5,000 ...	3	4	7	13
6,000 ...	3	5	8	15
7,000 ...	4	6	9	17
8,000 ...	4	6	10	20
9,000 ...	5	7	12	22
10,000 ...	6	8	13	25

The Risk of Ruin

The money-management programs discussed so far have a risk of ruin (total loss of your bankroll) between 1 and 2 percent, excluding the Kelly Criterion, which has 0-percent risk of ruin. Money-management programs for our teams usually have a 5-percent risk of ruin, which we believe is acceptable for team play.

Players who *overbet* are much more likely to lose their entire bankroll, no matter how skillful they are. The worst thing that can happen to a beginning player is to overbet and *win*. The experience will simply encourage overbetting. The player who has a $300 bankroll and bets as if it were a $1,000 bankroll, spreading bets from $3 to $20 with an average advantage of 1.4 percent, has a risk of ruin of 15 percent.

One promising player we know won $50,000 within four months even though in some instances he overbet. He was lucky this time and won. However, the same player later lost $50,000 in one month.

"It was a nightmare," he later admitted. "I played catch-up, but nothing worked. I couldn't buy a hand. It was a dark period, one that I shall never forget."

Consider the emotional impact that the loss of $50,000 would have on the average person. The young player sought professional counseling and stopped playing blackjack for several months.

"Blackjack had become too significant," he said. "I neglected things that were really important to me. But I'm lucky. I lost money that I had won. It could have been worse."

That young player has returned to blackjack. He is winning consistently once again and is adhering to a strict money-management program.

Now the Bad News

There's just one problem with these neatly structured betting schedules that we have presented in this chapter. If you follow them in the casinos in Nevada, you'll be recognized as a card counter and be barred, or else, in most cases, the dealer will shuffle up on you. So in the 1980s, you will bet with the count only infrequently.

Then why bother learning to bet with the count? Learn to bet with the count in order to learn the relationship of your maximum bet (based on your bankroll) to your betting advantage, i.e., the percentage of all money wagered that you can expect to win in the long run. Getting the money on the table will depend on your imagination and creativity. Jerry Patterson's Break the Dealer money-management program, in the following pages, deals with today's realities and obstacles—and shows you how to overcome those obstacles.

Spartan Simplicity

If the U.S. Army had a blackjack team, it would probably opt for the following money-management program because of its simplicity and uniformity. We recommend the following method for single-deck play only. It is a variation of a method by Koko Ita in his book, *21 Counting Methods to Beat 21*. When using it, you will appear to be flat-betting and parlaying your wins most of the time. You may be able to achieve a betting spread of 8–1, although not an aggressive or strong one.

Your opening bet should be either four or eight units (whatever your unit of betting is). You can disguise your play even more by mixing the colors of your chips, as discussed earlier. Although this method is structured, the idea is not to appear deliberate or methodical. Just remember that most floor personnel make two moves when observing suspected card counters. First, they observe the suspected counter from a distance. Then, they make a second inspection from close range. If you detect a floor person watching, simply revert to a defensive blackjack strategy: flat-bet the appropriate number of units until the attention subsides.

The procedure is illustrated in the following diagrams. As you will see, your bets will slowly increase, decrease, or stay the same, depending upon whether you have a plus or a minus true count, and on whether you won or lost the previous hand.

Previous Bet	Result of Hand	Current Count	Next Bet
1	WON	PLUS	2
		MINUS	2
	LOST	PLUS	2
		MINUS	1
2	WON	PLUS	4
		MINUS	4
	LOST	PLUS	2
		MINUS	1

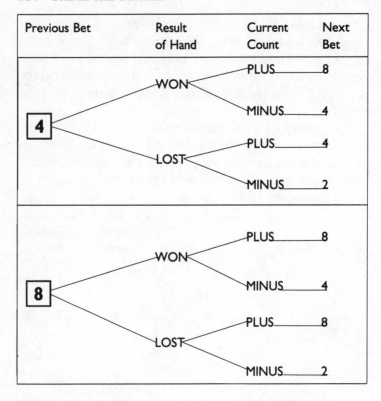

Previous Bet	Result of Hand	Current Count	Next Bet
4	WON	PLUS	8
		MINUS	4
	LOST	PLUS	4
		MINUS	2
8	WON	PLUS	8
		MINUS	4
	LOST	PLUS	8
		MINUS	2

Multiple-Deck Games—the Jerry Patterson Betting Strategy

In two-deck games with a favorable shuffle we recommend betting with the count (or approximately with the count) through parlaying wins and mixing the colors of chips. Open with a moderate bet to establish your credibility and range and don't overlook the significance of your subsequent "floor show" or act.

For shoe games in which a favorable shuffle is *not* used, we do not recommend betting with the count until the game has first proven itself. Does the count *mean* anything? Demand an approximate correlation between the count and what is occurring in the game—not only to your hand, but to the hands of the other players as well. On high plus counts, for example, is the dealer breaking with a small up-card or drawing to bizarre, multiple-card hands because of like-card clumping? If so, there is a correlation between the count and the cards being played. In blackjack terminology, the game has integrity. If, on the other hand, you have a high plus count yet you or the other players seem to be breaking with tens, the game does not have integrity, and you should consider leaving the table.

If the count is meaningful and you are winning, then bet with the count. If the count is not meaningful, but you are winning anyway, then *flat-bet* the game with a conservative, predetermined unit based on your bankroll. Your objective is to win three units. Keep playing until you have either won or lost a net total of three units. If you win two units, lose one, then win two more, you have achieved your goal—a net win of three units. Once you have won three units, increase your flat bet by 25 percent, and continue to flat-bet, using the count to play the hands and make insurance decisions. Here's an example:

You have decided to use a $10 unit for flat-betting purposes and have won three units. Twenty-five percent of $10 is $2.50, so your new unit is $12 (always round down). Continue to flat-bet now at $12 units.

With your new $12 unit, your next objective is to win three more units. If successful, your third plateau would be $15; your fourth plateau, $18; your fifth, $22. Here are some examples:

	$5 Unit	$10 Unit	$15 Unit	$25 Unit
First Plateau	$ 6	$12	$18	$31
Second Plateau	7	15	22	38

	$5 Unit	$10 Unit	$15 Unit	$25 Unit
Third Plateau	9	18	27	47
Fourth Plateau	11	22	33	58

This is fine as long as you're winning. But what happens if you lose three units? Leave the game and seek a new one, no matter if it's after three hands or on the fourth plateau. Do not be patient with any shoe game in which distribution may be restricted through an unfavorable shuffling procedure. The three-unit back-off is recommended for time-management as well as money-management reasons.

Chips can be used for bookkeeping purposes, if necessary, to remind you when to increase your bet or depart. Keep a win stack near your right hand and a loss stack near your left hand.

Betting Tips

What do floor personnel *really* look for while they are attempting to protect their games from card counters in Nevada (or in Atlantic City)? Four floor personnel with a combined casino experience of 46 years gave the following answers:

Anyone who is winning.

Anyone who makes a substantial bet while joining a game in progress.

Individuals with structured betting patterns.

Individuals who alter the number of hands they are playing.

"When I see someone winning, my immediate response is, 'What's going on?' " one floor person said. "I'll watch the game from a distance for a while. This gives me a good view of all the players as well as the dealer."

After several hands, the floor person said he may seek

additional surveillance, count down the deck, tell the dealer to speed up the game, or just dismiss the player and check back on the game from time to time.

House policy, however, is inconsistent toward suspected card counters. It is not only card counters who face the problem of being barred, but anyone who is a potential threat. Author A. Alvarez, in his book, *The Biggest Game in Town,* said that successful poker players when recognized are immediately banned from Las Vegas blackjack tables simply because it is assumed they have photographic memories.

"Erich Drache, for instance, was barred the first time he tried to play the game," Alvarez wrote. "He knew nothing about it but was betting heavily, because that is how he always bets. He had lost $5,000 in less than an hour, and then the shift changed. The new pit boss recognized him and stopped the game. 'This man gambles for a living,' he said. 'He can't play here.' "

One floor person told us that card counters are easy to identify. "Hell, card counters represent the majority of our business," the floor person said. "Who do they think they're kidding? They must think we're idiots. We don't bother small players much. Just the ones who are flagrant. A lot depends on how we've been doing."

According to our sources within the casino industry, there are two types of male counters:

Card counters under twenty-five wear Levi's, work pants, Army jackets, "two-dollar shirts," and are generally ungroomed, intense, callow, nervous, secretive, meticulous, and quiet. They do not speak to cocktail waitresses, dealers, or other players.

Card counters over twenty-five wear sport jackets, baggy and unpressed trousers, and resemble unemployed substitute teachers. They order coffee and fake conversations with cocktail waitresses, never taking their eyes off the cards. They palm or pocket chips.

Your credibility can be enhanced or destroyed by how you manage your money. If you're presenting yourself as a medium-range high roller (someone who bets fairly heavily), you're not doing much for that image if you open up a game by betting $5 a hand.

A more effective approach for a prospective high roller would be to flat-bet $100 off the top (in a game with a favorable shuffle). If you lose a few hands, fine. Lower your bet if the situation calls for it. This is what the average gambler would do. In the meantime, you've established the basis for a spread and the floor won't be surprised when they see another $100 bet in front of you. Remember the *typical* card counter opens with a relatively small bet.

Mixing the colors of your chips is an effective method for disguising your betting pattern. Consistently bet the same number of chips, but alter the colors according to the situation. On one hand, you might bet two green chips ($50) and four red chips ($20). This might be followed by four green chips ($100) and two red chips ($10). Eventually you might be able to incorporate a black chip ($100) or two into your color scheme. At all times, however, it will appear to a casual glance that you are betting about the same amount.

If you're portraying a high roller and getting a good game, don't try to pocket chips. Let them accumulate in front of you. A high roller doesn't pocket chips, so why should you? If you're betting small to middle range, it doesn't hurt to palm and pocket chips now and then. Don't be conspicuous or sneaky about it, though. Many gamblers pocket chips, so do it naturally, nonchalantly, and discreetly.

Points to Remember

1. In hands played, it's quality—not quantity—that matters in the modern game. This means be critical of the number of decks used, the type of shuffle, and the penetration.

2. Excessive losses can be minimized by concentrating on games with a favorable shuffle.

3. The key to becoming a consistent winning player is not necessarily how much you win, but oftentimes how little you lose. This means adhering to your predetermined stop-loss and playing within your bankroll.

4. Whatever the predetermined money-management strategy, it must be followed faithfully and accurately, without a single exception.

5. Good money management is related to good *time* management; in other words, don't squander your time inside casinos that offer unfavorable playing conditions.

6. Your bankroll should always be based on *real* money, never a fictional amount.

7. Your maximum bet should be equal to one-fiftieth of your bankroll and you should always plan your money-management strategy in advance—not inside a casino.

8. In games with a favorable shuffle, your major leverage is the *spread* between your minimum bet and your maximum bet. In Nevada, your skill at role-playing may determine that spread.

9. In Nevada single-deck and two-deck games, betting with the true count or the running count must be camouflaged to reduce the chances of being barred.

10. Based on our studies, the best betting method for multiple-deck games featuring the zone or stutter shuffle is flat-betting with gradual increments, as suggested in the Jerry Patterson Betting Strategy.

8 Casino Tips and Strategies

In this chapter we offer a number of tips on blackjack which will help you in your goal of being a winning player. Some of the strategies have to do with table etiquette and deportment, others with actual blackjack play. Not all of these may be necessary or right for you. Incorporate as many as you wish. But whether you adopt the strategies here or not, do keep in mind the reasons behind them. Your best weapon against the casinos is your own mind. Always pay attention to what is going on around you, and use *any* information you discover to your advantage. Dealers, other players, the type of shuffle, and the tables themselves all offer information to the blackjack player aware enough to notice and creative enough to use that information in terms of betting or even making a decision on whether or not to sit down to play a hand.

Look for Winning Situations

Size up the playing conditions of a casino or club *before* you sit down to play.

Note the number of decks, the type of shuffle, the number of rounds dealt (the penetration of the deck or shoe), as well as the house rules. Then ask yourself these two questions: (1) Does this house cater to "premiums" or "grinders"? and, (2) Is anyone winning?

It is disconcerting to walk into any house and detect little or no winning. After all, blackjack is a relatively close game. *Little or no winning may indicate an unfavorable house shuffle.* If so, do not play here—there are plenty of other casinos.

In small "grind" operations usually the best approach is to blend in with the other players as much as possible. Depict a local resident instead of an out-of-towner. Dress like the locals, even if this means dressing down, and place small bets. As a "local," you represent repeat business and this may encourage favorable treatment.

Overall, we don't recommend the smaller roadside stops.

It is generally a good idea, when playing in the smaller houses, not to call attention to yourself if you are doing well. One way to divert attention away from yourself is to emphasize that the dealer is *losing,* not that you're winning. Another way is to credit the decisions of other players by saying things like, "Gee, the dealer broke again." "Thanks, dealer, I sure needed help that time." "Good thing you drew that five, otherwise we would've lost."

Even in houses that use an unfavorable shuffle, pay attention to winning tables. There may be "friends of the house" in the game. If so, they are likely getting a favorable shuffle. At a Las Vegas casino, we found a lucrative two-deck game in which there was 100 percent winning among four players. After playing several hands, we learned that two of the players—both female—were friends of the floorman and that the dealer was not strip-shuffling, which was the regular house shuffle. (Strip shuffling is a very unfavorable shuffle for the player.)

In another situation, we found a game in which a regular customer was being given preferential treatment after he had lost $5,000 the two previous days. He sat down and played a few hands. As soon as he left the table with a $700 win, the dealer began strip-shuffling. We left shortly afterward.

In yet another situation, a "friend of the house" was told by a floor person to be "patient," although he was down by $3,000. The floor person intercepted a particular dealer and directed him to the table. The dealer has been with the club eight years and is known for his smooth, perfect shuffle. "If you can't beat this dealer, you can't beat blackjack," the floor person told the player, who recovered $2,000 of his loss within thirty minutes.

A Face in the Crowd

As we discussed in the chapter on shuffle-tracking, the problem with many card counters is that they look like card counters. Somber. Serious. Quiet. Meticulous. Even though, as a card counter, you are not relying on chance to win the game, you must at least pretend that you have thrown all caution to the wind and are playing the game at great risk. By projecting the image of a "gambler," which is after all the most desirable kind of customer for the casino, you will avoid attracting suspicious floor personnel to your table.

We suggest that you:

1. Be friendly and outgoing with everyone: players, dealers, floor personnel, and cocktail waitresses.

2. Be consistent with what you wear and the money you show. If you're dressing down, use small bills. If you're dressing up, flash big bills.

When you become a *master* at role-playing, you can even turn a loss to your advantage by letting everyone know that you have lost. Never be a silent loser. Seek sympathy. Be remembered as a loser rather than a winner. This can help you avoid being detected by the card-counter catchers.

Once when Eddie was getting nailed at a game of black-jack he attracted so much attention to himself that the next day, when he returned to the same table, both the dealer and a floor person remembered him well. His remarks of the previous day—"She's no dealer, she's a magician"; "It figures; I haven't won that hand since 1968"; "What are these—day-old cards? They smell"; "I'm gonna have to sell pencils after this"; "This place is worse than Atlantic City"—inspired the floor person to offer the dealer a bottle of breath sweetener to use on Eddie the second day if the game became rough for him again. "I see your friend is back," the floorman said, smiling. "This may come in handy later on."

Though it's acceptable to be remembered when you lose, it is not acceptable to be remembered when you win. But what are you going to do if you're caught in the act? Scowl or hover over your chips in an attempt to hide them?

Of course not.

"Look as if you are having a good time when you are winning," wrote Ian Andersen in his book, *Turning the Tables on Las Vegas*. "Most counters never change their facial expressions, win or lose—but the high roller is excited when winning."

Role-playing is essential in Nevada, and the best way to develop a good act is to study other people and emulate someone who impresses you. In Atlantic City, role-playing isn't quite as important because the casinos can't bar you, but they can still reshuffle, change the cards, or harass you in some other way, so it's advisable to disguise your abilities there, too. In creating a role or a casino personality, use your imagination, be original, and avoid clichés like the "drunk act."

Use disguises, but only if you can pull them off. One of Jerry Patterson's former students, who is a skillful player, makes himself conspicuous because the disguises he uses are so obvious. Floor personnel must have wondered why this man is wearing a disguise. Jerry sometimes uses disguises to hide the fact that he's a frequent player who wins most of the time. He creates a personality to match his disguise. He's been a screenwriter, a racetrack tout, an insurance salesman, and the president of an electronics firm. Sometimes he carries a homemade convention badge in case he decides to portray a conventioneer. But you have to wear the appropriate clothing. Most conventioneers, for example, don't go around in dungarees.

In the early days of Atlantic City, when players could be barred, one counter with good imagination and a sense of humor once used an "invisible friend" as a cover for his play. While he was involved in an ongoing conversation with the dealer and other players, the shoe suddenly became unusually rich. The card counter jumped to his feet and waved his arms as if he had just spotted a friend on the other side of the pit. "Susan! *Susan!* Over here," he shouted. In the meantime, he stacked another ten units in his bet while heads were turned looking for someone who did not exist. Use your imagination.

The best disguise for a man? Ask your dentist for several slabs of impression compound (wax disintegrates after about an hour) and make a mouthpiece for your lower jaw (similar to the mouthpiece worn by actor Marlon Brando in the motion picture *The Godfather*). Comb your hair differently or purchase a wig. If you don't wear eyeglasses, buy a pair with plain glass. But don't cut corners. The kind sold in dime stores have some magnification and could harm your eyes. Go to a cut-rate optometrist or eyeglass store. A suitable pair will cost between $25 and $50.

Women can dramatically alter their appearance with a creative change of hairstyle and wearing apparel.

If you're a professional player, tired of trudging along Fremont Street in Las Vegas or Virginia Street in Reno, try something absurd and bizarre for a change of pace. Be a cab driver or a bus driver. This will require a small investment for a hat and shirt, but we've never heard of a cab driver or bus driver being barred.

If you have a sense of humor, try carrying a cardboard bucket of quarters (the kind casinos make available for slot-machine players) to the table. You'll immediately be labeled an ignoramus (some players may even leave the table). Better yet, try placing a bet with a stack of quarters. After three or four hands, ask for a "keno runner."

Tips for Single-Deck Play

In searching for a single-deck game, your criteria should be, in order of priority:

1. A favorable shuffle.

2. Good penetration (a minimum of 32 cards played in a 52-card deck).

3. Favorable house rules.

Liberal house rules don't mean much if a single-deck game features an unfavorable shuffle and poor penetration. Never play games in which fewer than 32 cards are dealt. Make 32 your absolute minimum. The deeper the penetration, the more meaningful your count.

So, be greedy. Sometimes you can help penetration by playing an additional hand (on the average round, 2.7 cards are dealt per hand). If you and one other player are being dealt three rounds, this is an unacceptable game with about 24.3 cards. In this situation, try to improve penetration by going to two hands. The three-handed game will be dealt 32.4 cards, provided the dealer continues to deal three rounds. If the dealer cuts the game to two rounds (21.6 cards), you've worsened an unfavorable situation.

The following chart shows the number of cards you can expect to see in a single-deck game based on the number of hands and rounds. Remember, 32 cards is the absolute minimum. Anything inside the boxed area is unplayable.

ROUNDS							

NUMBER OF PLAYERS' HANDS

ROUNDS	1	2	3	4	5	6	7
1	5.4	8.1	10.8	13.5	16.2	18.9	21.6
2	10.8	16.2	21.6	28.0	32.4	37.8	43.2
3	16.2	24.3	32.4	40.5	48.6	—	—
4	21.6	32.4	43.2	—	—	—	—
5	27.0	40.5	—	—	—	—	—
6	32.4	48.6	—	—	—	—	—
7	37.8	—	—	—	—	—	—

In general, the best penetration for single-deck games is in Reno, and the worst is found at Lake Tahoe.

Tips for the Multiple-Deck Game

Do not play off new cards in multiple-deck games that feature a zone or stutter shuffle. This applies to all Atlantic City games and most casinos on the Las Vegas Strip using four or more decks. The like-card clumping will be devastating. Wait until the new cards have been shuffled for up to two hours. If the games are not in continuous play, you should wait even longer. Of course, the longer you wait, the better off you are. Scouting multiple-deck games toward the end of the shift is better than attempting to find a game at the beginning of a shift. Some casinos change cards in shoe games with each shift; others do not. The policies are inconsistent. If in doubt, ask a floor person what time the cards are changed. Old cards are easy to identify in Atlantic City during the summer months because salt-water air from the Atlantic Ocean warps them.

An ideal time to scout multiple-deck games with a zone or stutter shuffle is about two hours before the end of each shift in establishments that change cards. Pay attention to any evidence of winning because this may indicate an absence of like-card clumping, which is to be avoided. Dealer "wipeout" hands in which the dealer beats every player at the table *without a blackjack* are sometimes the result of like-card clumping. Be continuously aware of how the dealer is beating you, *particularly when a low card is showing*. Some examples of dealer "wipeout" could include:

    5,5,5,5
    6,5,5,5
    3,7,3,7
    3,A,A,A,3
    4,4,4,5
    6,7,8

Atlantic City Tips

Although they now have the authority to do so, most Atlantic City casinos do not reshuffle when players increase their bets substantially. Watch out for those that do.

The Golden Nugget Hotel & Casino has one of the most efficient security teams in Atlantic City and it does the majority of its serious surveillance from the sky (lookout points in the ceiling). Floor personnel usually keep low profiles.

Shuffles and "washes" (the manner in which new cards are introduced) are modified regularly in Atlantic City. Since 1982, we have documented twenty-eight shuffle modifications. Always look for a favorable shuffle.

Points to Remember

1. Before you play, evaluate a casino's blackjack game. Consider the number of decks, the type of shuffle, penetration or the number of rounds dealt, and the house rules. The lower the number of decks played, the better the game. But for multiple-deck games, get the best penetration you can find, preferably: one and one-half decks for two-deck games, three decks for four-deck games, and four decks for six-deck games. For an eight-deck shoe, don't settle for anything less than six decks. Do not play at casinos with unfavorable conditions.

2. Determine whether the casino caters to "premiums" or "grinders" and then plan your act, as well as your attack, accordingly.

3. Do you see any evidence of winning? If you don't, take another look at the house shuffle. If you see stutter shuffling and strip shuffling, you may want to look for another casino with a more favorable shuffle.

4. Attempt to blend in with the other customers. But when you lose, try to be remembered—it's a good future investment.

5. Be consistent with what you wear and the money you show, particularly in Nevada.

6. Role-playing is necessary in Nevada; be imaginative.

7. In multiple-deck games, do not play off fresh cards.

Scout games only after they have been in continuous play for at least two hours.

8. Monitor games for distribution to avoid games with excessive like-card clumping; remember, like-card clumping is usually the result of insufficient shuffling procedures; it can subvert the mathematics of blackjack.

9 The TARGET Method

The responsibility for change, therefore, lies with us. We must begin with ourselves, teaching ourselves not to close our minds prematurely to the novel, the surprising, the seemingly radical.
—ALVIN TOFFLER, *The Third Wave*

TARGET (*T*able, *R*esearch, *G*rading and *E*valuation *T*echnique) is a blackjack table selection method invented by Eddie Olsen that has been marketed by Jerry Patterson since 1982. Although it has provoked controversy because it does not have a mathematical basis, we consider TARGET to be the most significant blackjack tool since the invention of card counting.

TARGET identifies blackjack tables where the players have advantage over the house. TARGET works because it is not practical today to randomly shuffle four or more decks of cards or even single decks of cards. Biases develop that either favor the player or the dealer. TARGET players learn to detect the highly favorable player-biased tables.

Patterson welcomed the development of TARGET because so many of his card-counting students reported losing too many hands on high-count situations. He also noticed this phenomenon at many of their tables and began asking questions about why the count worked well at some tables and not at all at others. Unfortunately, none of the available blackjack research studies could answer these questions.

Blackjack research programs have used computers to study the game ever since card-counting was invented in 1962. Hundreds of millions of hands have been played under ideal conditions with a perfect random shuffle. Unfortunately, as mentioned many times herein, a random shuffle does not exist in the real world of casino play. A random shuffle is not likely, since even a single deck of cards must be shuffled up to thirty times to assure random distribution of the cards.

TARGET research on the effects of the nonrandom shuffle took place inside the casino. By observing and recording thousands of hands, and by *simulating* thousands more, Eddie Olsen, later with the help of Patterson's blackjack students and by collecting their data, discovered the characteristics of winning and losing tables. With various types of nonrandom shuffles, we were able to isolate and validate the fourteen TARGET factors that are the linchpins of the method.

Our research proved conclusively what we had suspected: that many dealer-biased games occur in high-count situations. This happens because of card clumps produced by certain nonrandom shuffles. For example, low card clumps can produce extremely high-count situations. The counter increases his bet in expectation that the missing high cards may never appear: a 20 or blackjack or a face card to his doubled 11. But because of extreme clumping, these high cards may never appear (residing behind the cut card) in this shoe. Or the high cards may be clumped, many showing up on the the same round with most players being dealt 20s and the dealer pulling a 20 also. These high cards are now out of play and not *randomly* available to the player when one is needed.

Like-card clumping can be devastating to a player. The reason is that the dealer hits his hand last. The player will stand on a stiff hand expecting the dealer to break. Playing into a low card clump, the dealer makes hand after hand breaking much less than the mathematically expected value (derived from a random shuffle study).

On the other hand, clumping can also be favorable to the player. Many dealer-breaking tables occur on neutral to negative counts. The clump may contain a surplus of rich cards which are contributing to the dealer-breaking activity.

You don't have to analyze or track shuffles to employ the TARGET Method. An understanding of fourteen simple factors is all that is needed to determine if the game is a player-biased game, and whether or not you should get into the game (or leave the game if the table is deteriorating and the card bias is changing).

Although TARGET can be played without counting cards, it works better if card-counting techniques are employed. But you must use a factor called table integrity to decide whether or not to bet up in a high-count situation.

Card-counters enjoy TARGET because it releases them from the constraints of traditional card-counting techniques. No more searching for those elusive head-to-head games; no more playing at odd hours when head-to-head games are supposedly available; no more worries about bad cut-card placement; biases detected by TARGET transcend the shuffle, so the effect of cut-card placement is reduced. The TARGET table entry techniques will get the card-counter into many more playable games.

TARGET is a short-term money-making technique. It does not work like traditional card-counting techniques where many hours of play may be required before the mathematics prevail and a player wins money. Through our empirical studies, we have determined that a TAR-GET player will win 80 percent of the time. Table selection is an investment decision. You expect to win at each and every table that you select. On those few occasions when a table does not offer a return on your investment, we teach you to cut your losses short and make a hasty departure. Something like a stop-loss technique that is used in stock market transactions.

TARGET's short-term advantages make it possible to play with a smaller bankroll than is required for traditional card counting techniques. This is because your chances of winning in any given session are much higher. We have experimented with a $100 casino bankroll and watched it appreciate to $500 on many occasions. The $100 was lost less than one time in five.

TARGET is a tool that is helpful for high rollers and gamblers even if they do not choose to invest the time to find the player-biased tables. All gamblers need information about when and how much to press their bets no matter at which table they are playing. TARGET gives them this information and provides them with a winning advantage without counting.

A Summary of the TARGET Method

The TARGET Method is based on the exploitation of the nonrandom shuffle. It is comprised of fourteen factors that the player uses to evaluate a table. The factors indicate whether or not the table is player-biased or dealer-biased. A player-biased table is one in which, because of favorable clumping, the players will win 50 percent or more of the hands. A dealer-biased table is one in which, because of unfavorable clumping, the dealer will win 50 percent or more of the hands.

Because TARGET is a proprietary method marketed by Jerry Patterson, we cannot disclose all of the TARGET factors in this book. But we will give you one example that you can use in your own play.

Consider the chip tray. Assume there are two empty columns in the tray with no chips. What does this mean? It could mean that players have come to this table, bought chips, played for a while and then left the table, neither winning much nor losing much. But it could also mean that the missing chips were won by the players. If this latter condition is the case, we may have a player-biased game. Of course, this one clue alone is not enough to give you conclusive evidence that this is a player-biased table. The TARGET player uses this factor, in conjunction with five or more of the other thirteen factors, to decide whether or not this table is an investment opportunity.

There are various styles of play associated with the TARGET Method. Some players scout for biased tables. They use the fourteen factors to decide whether or not to sit down and play. Others play at a table with only a few of the factors and, as long as they are not losing, wait for the other factors to develop. Some player-biased tables can be detected one or two shoes before the bias occurs.

Many TARGET players adopt the Partner Play Style. While one partner plays in a player-biased game, the other scouts for another table in the same casino. If they find a dealer-breaking table, both partners play in the same game.

TARGET works very well in blackjack tournaments. You can't choose your table in a tournament, but you can use the TARGET factors for your betting and playing decisions. One TARGET player won a recent tournament in Las Vegas, claiming more than $56,000 in prize money. Many others have placed quite high.

Blackjack Quiz

If you answer yes to any of the questions below, you should consider taking advantage of the money-making opportunities of the TARGET Method.

Have you ever sat at a blackjack table where the dealer was breaking a lot and you could do no wrong? You kept beating the dealer hand after hand?

☐Yes   ☐No

Were you ever $100 or more ahead while playing black-jack but did not leave the table when the cards turned against you? You gave all your profits back and then some?

☐Yes   ☐No

As a card counter, have you ever lost hand after hand in a very high-count situation with your maximum bet out and seen your trip's profits go down the tubes?

☐Yes   ☐No

Have you ever won hand after hand with your minimum bet out? How much more would you have made if you could have known the dealer would keep on breaking?

☐Yes   ☐No

Are you a would-be card counter who practiced at home but could never master counting? Does winning without counting appeal to you?

☐Yes   ☐No

Have you ever watched a blackjack player making a tremendous amount of money with seemingly little effort? Picture yourself in his shoes taking the money off the table. With TARGET this is possible.

Please see Appendix A for an outline of Jerry Patterson's TARGET Instructional Program.

10 The Psychology of Success

Whether you think you can, or think you can't . . . you're right.
—HENRY FORD

Through the years, we have found that players with negative attitudes—no matter how skillful and talented—do not develop into successful blackjack players over the long term. On the other hand, players who feel successful, who have confidence in their ability to win, often *are* more successful. While attitude certainly does not influence the cards that are dealt to you at a blackjack table, attitude does affect your decisions, judgment, and self-management. In this chapter we present the training program that we require all of our team players to undergo.

The twenty-one-day program features accelerated learning and self-relaxation methods designed to help you achieve your goals, realize your potential, and develop a successful winning attitude.

Does our program really work? A number of our players have reported higher win rates after incorporating the program into their daily lives. One player, a psychologist, claims, "A winning attitude, a positive self-image, and the mental ability to attack the casinos are sixty-five percent of the game."

Our program should be used on a daily basis. Researchers have found that people who are exposed to material only one time will remember a mere 2 percent of that material after two weeks, while people exposed to the same material on six consecutive days will remember up to 65 percent two weeks later. Throughout this chapter, we ask that you maintain an open, affirmative mind.

On a short-term basis, success at blackjack can be deceptive. Often a successful player will lose a number of hands in a row, or may lose his or her first outing or first several outings to the casinos. There is an element of luck, too, to the game. A successful player is one who wins money in the long run—not the player who wins $200 one night, only to lose $300 over the succeeding nights. Don't allow blackjack to distort your values and goals. Determine its place in your life and keep it there. If it's a source of supplementary income, do not allow it to become more than it is. However, if you are a professional player, don't minimize blackjack and allow it to become less than it is.

Success in blackjack, as in all fields of endeavor, requires study, hard work, a positive mental attitude, a burning desire to succeed, and the will to persevere even after defeat.

A positive self-image is the most important attribute a player can have. It is not possible for you to be a winning blackjack player unless you *see* yourself a successful player. Blackjack, like other forms of competition, is really *two* games, instead of one. The "outer" game is the one that is waged against the casinos. The "inner" game is the one that takes place within ourselves.

The Twenty-one-Day Program

Do not attempt any of the exercises in the twenty-one-day Break the Dealer program until you have familiarized yourself with the entire chapter. To optimize the effectiveness of the exercises, we also ask that you monitor all the information that you digest. In other words, be just as mindful of your mental diet as you are of your nutritional diet. Here are some suggestions:

Language. Turn your world upside down. Think in terms of "I can" instead of "I can't"; "today" instead of "tomorrow."

The Media. Limit your television viewing to positive, helpful programs. Think in terms of positive and negative and eliminate the negative. Avoid television news and commercials. Listen to inspiring, upbeat music. In newspapers, magazines, and books, think of every story as being either positive or negative; avoid reading negative stories.

People. Avoid pessimists, cynics, and people with a multitude of problems. Search out and mingle with winners.

Environment. Skip nightclubs and taverns. View the positive in life. Spend time with nature.

The first exercise in your daily program is autogenics. The word "autogenics" comes from the Greek-derived "autogenous," meaning "self-produced." It is a method for stress control through self-relaxation. Chess players have used it since 1971. Listening to music with a slow tempo, especially baroque music—which is performed at a tempo which corresponds to the rhythm of a resting human heart—while doing this exercise can increase the benefits to you.

First, assume a comfortable position. If you are sitting in a chair, sit upright and let your head hang slightly forward with your arms hanging at your sides. Plant your feet comfortably with your toes turned slightly outward. If you are reclining, your head should be slightly elevated.

Your arms should be at your sides, slightly bent at the elbows, palms down. Your legs should not touch each other; your feet should be pointing slightly outward.

1. Start a *gentle* sustained cycle of deep breathing without straining, keeping your mouth closed. The purpose of the breathing exercise is to slow your body and mental rhythms. Your breathing should be rhythmic. Continue for one minute.

2. Inhale slowly as you count to four; hold your breath to the count of four; exhale slowly as you count to four; pause to the count of four. Repeat this pattern four times. Relax. Then, using a count of six, repeat this pattern four more times. Relax.

Close your eyes. Concentrate on the music and do the self-relaxation exercise that follows. Use your imagination. Make an attempt to "feel" each exercise, without forcing it. Note: This exercise—or any self-relaxation exercise—should not be attempted while driving a motor vehicle.

Focus on your arms. Feel a gentle warmth moving from your hands to your elbows and from your elbows to your shoulders. Concentrate on your right arm, then your left arm; finally, both of your arms. Say to yourself, "Both of my arms are warm." Now focus on your legs, feeling gentle warmth moving from your feet to your thighs. Concentrate on your right leg, then your left leg; finally, both of your legs. Say to yourself, "Both of my legs are warm." Pause for a moment. Now feel the gentle warmth settling in both your arms and legs. Say to yourself, "My arms and legs are warm."

Repeat the above steps, but this time feeling warmth and *heaviness* in your arms and legs. Go slowly; don't force it. Conclude the exercise by thinking of coolness, and then of coolness and weightlessness. Imagine yourself floating on a cloud. Your breathing should be relaxed and effortless, your heartbeat calm and regular.

Do not end the session abruptly. Open your eyes slowly and stretch gradually, flexing your muscles. Notice how fresh and alert you feel. In the beginning, many people have difficulty experiencing the warmth and heaviness sensations. Don't worry about this—you will improve with practice.

After you have achieved a state of relaxation, use self-affirmation (positive imaging) to implant suggestions and script your own success. With such self-made scripts, you are consciously taking control of the unconscious suggestions that will shape your future.

Instead of speaking aloud to yourself, you may want to record your affirmative statements on a cassette tape and play it while you're listening to baroque music. In either case, you should focus on the music and not on the voice or statements. Your unconscious mind will hear and record the tape. The affirmations you make should be short, four or five words, and spaced about four seconds apart, spoken in alternating tones—first in an affirmative tone, then as a command, and finally, softly, suggestively.

Such "affirmations" should not be predications ("I will win"), but rather present-tense statements: "I am a winner." Phrase your affirmations as if you are already in possession of the desired characteristic or trait. Never use negative phrasing. The brain cannot focus on two concepts at once. Say to yourself, "I am a winner," rather than "I am not a loser."

Speak with emotion and feeling in saying these affirmatives aloud to yourself. Every shred of information is received by the brain. The right half of the brain, the unconscious, makes no judgment on the validity of the input and cannot distinguish fact from fiction. Think of it as a rehearsal for the person you want to become. During the first seven days of the program, it is best to stick to *one subject* at a time. For example, if you wish to improve your card-counting ability, you might make a tape of the following statements:

"I am a successful card counter."

"When I count cards, I never lose the count."

Through repetition of such suggestions, your unconscious mind will alert your conscious mind to this new image. Your mind will orchestrate your improvement automatically.

Use affirmative statements to improve the way you manage yourself while playing blackjack. Here are some suggestions:

"My mind is clear and alert."

"I have faith and confidence in my skills."

"I am in control of my emotions."

"I understand the play of others."

"Money management is second nature with me."

"My basic strategy skills are improving."

"I'm oblivious of excessive noise and clatter."

"I'm a winner."

Visualization exercises can be used in conjunction with self-relaxation or for the reinforcement of blackjack goals. Mental pictures also give you an opportunity to "practice" skills and "meet" challenges.

We are not suggesting that forming mental pictures will get you more blackjacks or winning hands. But by mentally picturing yourself as a successful player—visualizing the play of your hands, your money management, and your table departure—you can improve your casino play and your "inner" game. You'll make fewer mistakes. The use of imagination through visualization cannot be under-estimated.

Putting It to Work

Do your exercises in a comfortable room where you will not be disturbed. We suggest doing the exercises in succession before retiring, but some people prefer splitting them up during the day because of their life-styles and work schedules. For this reason, a Daily Success Diary that can be used as a checklist is included in this chapter.

On the Daily Success Diary is a space for a "daily success." Use one or two words to record a success each day, no matter how insignificant. It could be a blackjack win or some other success unrelated to the game. Keep in mind that you have an obligation to seek out and achieve at least one success per day. Before you retire, look over the diary and replay that success in your mind. Evaluate each day with either two pluses (+ +) or one plus (+), never a minus.

Also included in this chapter is a Self-Inventory, which is intended to compare your pre-casino and post-casino dispositions. The comparisons may give you ideas for affirmations or self-statements. We suggest that you do the Self-Inventory for three casino trips or as needed.

Here is an example of the inner and outer game of blackjack at work, as described in a first-person account by Jerry Patterson:

One casino in Atlantic City decided to pump up business with a four-deck game in December 1984. For one month it offered the best game in Atlantic City history, and using an alias, I was a nightly player. Their special card-count unit responded by assigning a countercatcher to regularly shadow me; after a while, we became friends of sorts.

I learned the ground rules quickly. The casino would allow me a 3–1 betting spread without shuffling up. Once, I forgot myself and went from $50 to $200. From my "shadow" in the aisle came the order, "Shuffle up."

After the bait had been set and the tables were full, the casino reverted to a double-stutter shuffle and the game turned vicious, but was still worth scouting. One night, I was playing two hands and had $200 bets on each one: two stiffs, a 15 and a 16. The dealer showed a 10. I had a true count of 6 and decided to stand on both hands. The dealer broke. "Just like hitting a home run," I said, turning to my shadow.

Overall, it hadn't been a good night. Misleading counts and opportunities. Too many mirages and I was losing. My shadow seemed to be enjoying it and this annoyed me. "Tough game, isn't it?" my shadow said. I drew two 5s, doubled down, and caught another 5. "Maybe you should have split those 5s," the shadow said. Inside a room for high-stakes players, I paused at a $100 table. "You don't belong in that game," the shadow said. Inside the main casino, I stopped at another game and my shadow walked right into me. Now my anger was beginning to swell.

I stopped looking for a game and walked into the lobby. Forget the shadow and concentrate on the game, I thought, taking a coffee break. The inner game and the outer game, I reminded myself. No matter what, I would win the inner game.

Back inside the casino, I paused at a craps table. It's time to play, I thought. The diversion was as refreshing as a cold shower. No more anger. Soon afterward, it was back to the blackjack tables and now I had two shadows. I ignored them and found my game. "Aren't you betting over your head?" one shadow quipped. I ignored the comment and concentrated on the game.

The chips began to build in front of me, but I ignored them. Total concentration on each hand. I had blanked the shadows and their comments from my mind.

I looked for my shadows after cashing out. They were nowhere in sight. Oh well, I thought, and took the escalator to the Boardwalk. The night air and the smell of the Atlantic Ocean were invigorating. I left the casino with a $7,000 win. I had won both the inner game and the outer game. It had been a good night.

The daily program with recommended sequence and estimated time:
1. Gentle breathing exercise, 2 minutes.
2. Autogenic exercises (with baroque-period music), 10 minutes.
3. Suggestion or affirmation exercises (with baroque-period music), 10 minutes.
4. Visualization, 5 minutes.
5. Daily Success Diary, 1 minute.
6. Self-Inventory, when appropriate.

The daily commitment is about 30 minutes, or 3½ hours a week. For twenty-one days, make the Break the Dealer program part of your daily life; look upon it as an investment in your blackjack-playing future. We are confident that you will realize tangible, measurable results.

Recommended Reading

Self-development or self-help books can be a good source for reinforcement. We have covered the field and recommend the following:

Hill, Napoleon, *Think and Grow Rich*, Wilshire Book Co., Hollywood, CA.

Maltz, Maxwell, *Psycho-Cybernetics*, Simon & Schuster, Inc., New York, NY.

Mandino, Og, *The Greatest Salesman in the World*, Bantam Books, Inc., New York, NY.

Ostrander, Sheila, and Lynn Schroeder, *Superlearning*, Dell Publishing Co., Inc., New York, NY.

Schuller, Robert H., *Tough Times Never Last, But Tough People Do!*, Bantam Books, Inc., New York, NY.

Stone, W. Clement, *The Success System That Never Fails*, Simon & Schuster, Inc., New York, NY.

Waitley, Denis, *Seeds of Greatness*, Fleming H. Revell Co., Old Tappan, NJ.

Ziglar, Zig, *See You at the Top*, Pelican Publishing Co., Gretna, LA.

Recommended Listening

Audiocassette tapes are another source for reinforcement and can be used to turn such "dead-time" periods as driving a car into learning and self-improvement sessions. The leading manufacturer of audiocassette tapes is the Nightingale-Conant Corporation, which has produced such best-selling albums as *Lead the Field* by Earl Nightingale, *The Psychology of Winning* by Denis Waitley, and *Possibility Thinking* by Robert H. Schuller.

Catalogs will be sent upon request from the following companies:

The Nightingale-Conant Corp., 3730 West Devon Avenue, Chicago, IL 60659.

Listen USA, Audio Cassette Collection, Post Office Box 396, Old Greenwich, CT 06870.

The Zig Ziglar Corp., 13642 Omega at Alpha, Dallas, TX 75234.

Denis Waitley, Inc., Post Office Box 197, Rancho Santa Fe, CA 92067.

Superlearning, Inc., 450 Seventh Avenue, Suite 500, New York, NY 10123.

Learning Alternatives, Post Office Box 405, East Rutherford, NJ 07073.

Books on Tape, Post Office Box 7900, Newport Beach, CA 92658.

Your Daily Success Diary

This page represents a three-week checklist for the use of breathing, autogenics, suggestopedics, visualization, and baroque-period music in your Break the Dealer program. Space is also provided for a "daily success." Evaluate each day with either two pluses (+ +) or one plus (+), never a minus.

Today's Date	Breathing	Autogenics	Suggestopedics	Visualization	Music	Today's Success	Evaluation

Your Self-Inventory

The purpose of your Self-Inventory is to compare your pre-casino disposition with your post-casino disposition. This will help you call your attention to your attitudes and performance. You may or may not detect areas that you wish to correct through the use of suggestopedics. Use the inventory for three casino trips, rating yourself on a scale from 5 (excellent) to 1 (poor).

PRE-CASINO
EVALUATION

POST-CASINO
EVALUATION

I __ 2 __ 3 __ .... Concentration ...... I __ 2 __ 3 __

I __ 2 __ 3 __ .... Perseverance .... I __ 2 __ 3 __

I __ 2 __ 3 __ .... Discipline .... I __ 3 __ 3 __

I __ 2 __ 3 __ .... Accuracy .... I __ 2 __ 3 __

I __ 2 __ 3 __ .... Self-Image .... I __ 2 __ 3 __

I __ 2 __ 3 __ .... Attitude .... I __ 2 __ 3 __

I __ 2 __ 3 __ .... Blackjack Skills ...... I __ 2 __ 3 __

I __ 2 __ 3 __ ... Did you use autogenics?

I __ 2 __ 3 __ ... Did you use suggestions and affirmations?

The outcome of the "inner" game +/− ... I __ 2 __ 3 __
The outcome of the "outer" game +/− ... I __ 2 __ 3 __

11 The World's Shortest Blackjack Course

It is beginning to dawn on us that our obsessive emphasis . . . on progressively finer and finer measurement of smaller and smaller problems, leaves us knowing more and more about less and less.
—ALVIN TOFFLER, *The Third Wave*

The simplified basic strategy and the Patterson Short-Count included in this chapter are not intended for the serious player. They are intended to serve as survival tools for the recreational player who does not wish to spend the time or energy in mastering the complexities of the game. They can be learned in several hours.

The simplified basic strategy used with the Patterson Short-Count will give you a slight advantage in the single-deck game, but as presented here, the short-count is not recommended for multiple-deck play.

There are just ten rules to learn in the simplified basic strategy. They cover the hands most frequently played and should be learned in the order in which they are presented. The rules can be used for all games, although minor errors occur in multiple-deck games. These errors can be corrected by referring to the appropriate basic-strategy chart in Chapter 3.

The Simplified Basic Strategy

Hitting/Standing Rules:

1. Stand on 12 through 16 if the dealer's up-card is 2 through 6; otherwise hit.

2. Hit until you have a hard total of 17 or more if the dealer's up-card is 7 through A.

3. Hit A,2 through A,6 (for exceptions, see Rule 7); stand on A,7 through A,9.

Double-Down Rules:

4. Double on 11 when the dealer's up-card is 2 through 10.

5. Double on 10 when the dealer's up-card is 2 though 9.

6. Double on 9 when the dealer's up-card is 3 through 6.

7. Double on A,2 through A,7 when the dealer's up-card is 4 through 6.

Rules for Splitting Pairs:

8. Always split As and 8s.

9. Never split 10s, 5s, or 4s.

10. Split 2s, 3s, 6s, 7s, and 9s when the dealer's up-card is 4 through 6.

After you have mastered the ten basic rules, you may want to add these refinements:

11. Hit 12 if the dealer's up-card is 2 or 3.

12. Hit A,7 when the dealer's up-card is 9, 10, or A.

The Patterson Short-Count

All card-counting systems are information-gathering techniques. They enable a player to evaluate the "richness"—high-card density—of the unplayed cards. When high cards outnumber low cards, the odds of winning shift from the house to the player, and this is when a card counter exploits the situation by increasing his or her bet.

The Patterson Short-Count does not differ dramatically from traditional techniques except for its simplicity. It is unique because the average person can learn to use it accurately within several hours, mindful that he or she is sacrificing effectiveness for simplicity. Serious players who want a stronger count should use the high-low system as described in Chapter 4.

In the Patterson Short-Count, only the five low cards are tracked—2s, 3s, 4s, 5s, and 6s. The key to the Patterson Short-Count is the Pivotal Number, or PN, which is based on the number of hands being played. To determine the PN, simply count the number of hands being dealt, including the dealer's hand. For example, the PN in a game with four players would be five, including the dealer's hand. If one of the four players was playing two spots, the PN would be *six*.

In single-deck play, count the number of low cards (2s, 3s, 4s, 5s, 6s) played in each round. Compare that number with the Pivotal Number (PN). If it is equal to or less than the PN, you do not have an advantage for the next hand and you should not increase your bet. However, if your count of the low cards exceeds the pivotal number, you have an advantage and should increase your bet accordingly. The small-card excess will determine the additional number of units you will bet for the following hand as illustrated in the following table:

Number of units previously bet	Surplus of low cards over Pivotal Number	Units to be bet on the next hand	Increase
1	1	2	1
1	2	3	2
1	3	4	3
1	4	5	4

You do not have to carry the count from one hand to the next. Count each hand only as it is played.

Remember, the Patterson Short-Count will give you an advantage whenever the number of small cards exceeds the Pivotal Number by one. This will not be the case in multiple-deck play. Our only recommendation for the multiple-deck game would be a combination of the simplified basic strategy and the high-low counting system, which is described in Chapter 4.

12 Computer vs. Computer

If you don't know where you're going, you may wind up some-place else.

—LAWRENCE J. PETER

Electronic Blackjack

Ken Uston was the first known player to use a concealed microcomputer at a blackjack table when he introduced a black box named "George" to team play in 1977. "George" and his brothers had an 80-percent success rate and Uston envisioned a $3 million year until authorities confiscated one of the contraptions at a casino in Reno. Although federal authorities ruled that "George" was not a cheating device, Uston returned to straight blackjack. And eventually, both Nevada and New Jersey prohibited the use of microcomputers at the blackjack table.

In 1980 the casino industry itself turned to the computer when the New Jersey Casino Control Commission and the Atlantic City Hotel Association contracted Econ, Inc., a Princeton, New Jersey, computer firm, to assemble a blackjack-simulation model to analyze player performance as well as rules and procedures, including the early surrender rule.

"Everyone was suspicious of us," a former Econ official

recalled. "The casinos thought we were working for the state and the state thought we were working for the casinos. The players? They thought we had sold out to everyone."

Data from the simulation of fifty million hands convinced the Casino Control Commission that early surrender should be eliminated. The success of the Econ researchers proved to the casino industry that computer simulations could work to their advantage.

The blackjack-simulation model could analyze the effectiveness of any house rule or procedure. It could also simulate the play of different types of players, from card counters to basic-strategy players to the general public. It could evaluate player mix, betting strategies, and the performance of any shuffling procedure.

In the beginning, Econ, Inc., couldn't handle all of the blackjack simulations on its own computer, so the state's computer in Trenton, New Jersey, was used. "The amount of computer time we needed was incredible," a former Econ employee said. "Blackjack ate up so much computer time that there were nights the state police couldn't even make a routine check on a license-plate number."

Although early surrender became a forgotten issue, Econ, Inc., still had the blackjack-simulation model and its valuable data bases. It performed more work for the casino industry, some of it piecemeal. There was a study on complimentary services. Another study on high rollers. Performance studies on the Bart Carter Shuffle. Studies on shuffles for six-deck and eight-deck games and other evaluations designed to protect casino bankrolls.

Where Are the Casinos Going?

Electronic shuffling devices could end any debate about a forthright shuffle. One continuous-shuffling device has been designed by Joel Greenberg, president of Princeton Synergetics, Inc. Greenberg said his contraption would speed up blackjack play by about 25 percent and reduce a card counter's earnings to about ten cents an hour.

The machine would eliminate the need for a traditional discard rack because cards that had been played would be fed right back into the machine. Greenberg said he designed the machine "to stop the Ken Ustons of the world."

Would the public shun a machine?

Greenberg said he didn't believe the public would object. But we believe such devices would have a significant impact on blackjack's popularity, which is based on a belief that the game can be beaten. Machines or automation would undermine that belief.

13 Yesterday, Today, and Tomorrow

There is a fifth dimension beyond that which is known to man . . . it lies between the pit of man's fears and the summit of his knowledge. This is the dimension of imagination.
—ROD SERLING, *The Twilight Zone*

Frankly, we *prefer* the challenges of the modern game and do not lament the passing of blackjack's "candy-store" days, when playing conditions were more favorable to the traditional card counter.

Countermeasures implemented by New Era casino operators to thwart skillful players should be regarded as puzzles that can be solved, not insurmountable handicaps. Besides, those countermeasures are invariably withdrawn from the games and replaced by new and different ones.

Imagination is important in blackjack. If it is necessary to develop a countermeasure to compensate for a countermeasure, you simply do it. Such was the case in 1982 when we faced the possibility of widespread use of Blackjack II, the twelve-deck game dealt from a double shoe. For that game, we abandoned traditional blackjack methods and developed what we called the "dual count." The situation demanded it.

When we were confronted with an array of games fea-

159

turing continuous shuffles, including the Bart Carter Shuffle, we again needed a new tool. Eventually we developed a rather complicated tracking system we named the "wave count."

Both Blackjack II and the Bart Carter Shuffle were short-lived. But the concepts introduced in *Break the Dealer* are innovations based on similar new developments in the casinos. We believe our innovations will have long-term value against most casino countermeasures since the most effective countermeasures have hinged on the shuffle.

Shuffle-tracking will not result in a Macedonian fortune. It may not even help you win $500 a day. But it is just as much of an offensive tool as card counting. Selecting a favorable shuffle, on the other hand, should be considered a defensive tool; it may help to minimize your losses. It will certainly keep you out of outlandish "house" games. Both of these concepts are *supplementary* tools; they are not substitutes for card counting and basic strategy.

Throughout *Break the Dealer* we have stressed two tools already in your possession: originality and imagination. They are the most valuable of all tools; they always have been and they always will be.

Yesterday's Heroes

Every major blackjack achiever has exhibited originality and imagination, and Kenneth S. Uston is no exception.

In his early days, Uston's flamboyance flabbergasted floor personnel and earned him a variety of nicknames, including the "Wandering Jew" and the "Mad Bomber." Uston was a daredevil, an Evel Knievel without a motorcycle, jogging through pits, scrambling around stools, and pushing aside other players in what seemed to be a frenzied attempt to put money on the table.

Later, Uston and his mentor, "Al Frencesco," improved a team concept, used by a Texan known as "Mr. B," to develop the first "Big Player" team. And Uston's teams went on to win a reported $4.5 million between 1974 and 1979.

In the early 1980s, most casinos had banned Uston from their tables. Uston continued various legal battles based on his barrings, winning a significant New Jersey decision. Then in 1985 he attempted an ambitious comeback with three blackjack teams.

Originality and imagination have also earmarked the career of Stanley R. Sludikoff, publisher of *Gambling Times* magazine. One of blackjack's earliest big-name players, Sludikoff is also known as "Stanley Roberts," author of *The Beginner's Guide to Winning Blackjack*, *The Gambling Times Guide to Blackjack*, and *Winning Blackjack*. During the early 1970s he helped popularize blackjack by appearing on more than two hundred radio and television programs, including *What's My Line?* and *To Tell the Truth*.

Sludikoff's editorials are often hard-hitting, blunt, and sprinkled with "Sludikoffisms." In explaining his dual identity to his readers, Sludikoff wrote: "When I write, I will be Stanley Roberts; when I publish, I will be Stanley R. Sludikoff. There's no mystery in it, and virtually everyone in the industry knows who I am." Beneath his listing in *Who's Who in America* is a favorite Sludikoff quotation: "The challenge of being alive lies in the development of one's maximum potential."

Ian Andersen, Julian H. Braun, Peter A. Griffin, Lance Humble, Lawrence Revere, Arnold Snyder, Edward O. Thorp, and Stanford Wong have all made important contributions to the field of blackjack.

"Ian Andersen" is a professional gambler, a world-class

blackjack player, and the author of *Turning the Tables on Las Vegas,* a book which stresses the importance of self-discipline and camouflage.

Julian H. Braun, an instructor at the IBM Advanced Education Center in Chicago, was the first person to compute an exact basic strategy. He has contributed important data to the field of blackjack research and is the author of *How to Play Winning Blackjack,* published in 1980.

Peter A. Griffin, professor of mathematics at California State University, is perhaps blackjack's foremost theoretician. His book, *The Theory of Blackjack,* is considered the *Beowulf* of blackjack literature.

"Lance Humble," professor of psychology at the University of Toronto, is really Igor Kusyshyn, a psychologist who has been quoted in several blackjack books. Founder of the International Blackjack Club, author of *Blackjack Gold,* and coauthor of *The World's Greatest Blackjack Book,* he also markets his own playing strategies through International Gambling, Inc.

"Lawrence Revere," a former pit boss and dealer, developed the "Revere Advanced Point Count" with Julian H. Braun, a strategy which has been used by a number of successful players, including Ken Uston. He also wrote *Playing Blackjack as a Business.*

"Arnold Snyder" publishes *Blackjack Forum,* the newsletter, and has authored three highly regarded books since 1980—*The Blackjack Formula, Blackjack for Profit,* and *Blackbelt in Blackjack.* Also known as "Bishop Snyder," he is the founder of the First Church of Blackjack.

Edward O. Thorp, a professor of mathematics, wrote the 1962 bestseller *Beat the Dealer.* A consultant to several institutions, Thorp is also president of a management company and chairman of a securities corporation.

"Stanford Wong" is the author of *Winning Without*

Counting, Blackjack in Asia, Professional Blackjack, and a booklet, *Blackjack Secrets.* He also publishes two newsletters, *Current Blackjack News* and *Winning Gamer,* and is the developer of "Party Blackjack," a program for IBM personal computers.

Blackjack Tomorrow

Overall, the 1970s were boom years for the gambling industry, which expanded to Atlantic City in 1978. Some of the best card counters in the country also expanded their play to Atlantic City. Joel H. Sterns, attorney for Resorts International Hotel, Inc., stated the industry's stance for the eighties in 1981:

"Certainly no person has a vested right to win at a casino game. Conversely, no business should be forced to sell a nonnecessity, entertainment service to a class of patrons at a guaranteed loss. Such thinking is contrary to the fundamental concept of casino gaming."

Steve Norton, executive vice-president of Resorts International, expressed his concern to *The Wall Street Journal:* "Blackjack has become a game of skill here, not a game of chance. We believe if we're going to build a big expensive casino, we should have the mathematical advantage in every game."

Casino executives said the problem could be handled if dealers were allowed to simply shuffle-up when card counters were suspected, but the Casino Control Commission refused to consider the suggestion. Instead, it hired a consulting firm to study other alternatives.

At the 1981 National Conference on Gambling and Risk Taking at Stateline, Nevada, blackjack author Stanford Wong attempted to reason with the casino industry:

"It is a fact that the casinos must make a profit on

blackjack in order to offer the game. I am a businessman myself; I understand the need to make a profit. However, the casinos do not need to have an edge over every single customer in order to show an overall profit."

Stanley R. Sludikoff, publisher of *Gambling Times* magazine, warned: "To try to change the game so it cannot be beaten will be a direct assault upon the principle of why the game flourishes."

As far as the casino industry is concerned, the question of whether or not to preserve aspects of blackjack that make it a game of skill isn't open to debate. Luck, not skill, should govern the outcome of all casino games, is the dominant viewpoint. Las Vegas' remarkable recovery from the 1983 recession dramatized blackjack's effectiveness as a marketing tool to attracting customers to the casinos, thereby prolonging the survival of single-deck and two-deck games. New Jersey casinos do not enjoy the same marketing freedom that the Nevada casinos have because of what some executives claim are excessive state regulations. The government's power was particularly evident in 1985 when the New Jersey Casino Control Commission waited until Hilton Hotels Corp. had completed a $300-million casino before it rejected its application for a license. The corporation promptly sold its facility to Donald Trump, but the decision of the Casino Control Commission to deny a license tarnished New Jersey's standing in the gambling industry and weakened its marketing opprtunities. "I think New Jersey went and shot itself in the foot," said one observer in the industry.

Golden Nugget, Inc., canceled plans to build a second casino-hotel in Atlantic City, blaming soft growth rates and announcing it would absorb a $15-million loss on the $300-million project. While market analysts were losing their enthusiasm for Atlantic City, New Jersey officials attempted to create confidence by announcing plans for a railway system.

"The city has got to get back into the blackjack business," one Nevada executive said. "It has to lure back the same players it tried to chase away in the beginning."

Atlantic City's marketing options are limited. Bus programs for slot-machine players—the major marketing thrust of the early 1980s—reached a saturation point. Without airline and railway facilities, it is not likely to become a regular site for major conventions. Atlantic City must market its table games. And it must market blackjack games that are competitive with Nevada.

The bottom line is that the outlook for blackjack has never been better because of the two-state rivalry. If the Atlantic City games improve, and they most certainly will, the Nevada games too will improve.

Still reeling from the 1983 recession, Las Vegas houses showcased additional single-deck and two-deck games in 1985 and the competition was particularly evident among the Dunes Hotel and Casino, the Tropicana Hotel & Country Club, the Riviera Hotel & Casino, and Caesars Palace Hotel & Casino.

In Atlantic City, there must be a return to the more favorable four-deck games. At present only six-deck and eight-deck games exist. By the late 1980s, even single-deck and two-deck games are not unlikely in New Jersey, particularly if another state legalizes casino gambling. This would require changes in the regulations either to permit hand-held games (presently all blackjack games in New Jersey must be dealt from a shoe) or to authorize the use of hand-held shoes. But a single-deck game, even at high-stakes tables, would improve business volume during the slow winter months.

Furthermore, state and local government must improve

transportation facilities to and from Atlantic City. Without them, Atlantic City is not a favorable site for major national conventions or year-round tourist trade.

A National Coalition

Because of the highly individual nature of blackjack players, the blackjack community is a divided community comprising unique individuals with differing skills, disciplines, and viewpoints. We believe a new era of cooperation among professional players, mathematicians, authors, and blackjack enthusiasts would be in the game's best interest. We do not propose that individuals modify or compromise their beliefs or sense of fair criticism. What we do propose is the creation of a national blackjack coalition that would be in each individual's best interest.

Left alone and given a choice, the casino industry is more likely to eliminate those aspects of blackjack that lend themselves to skill. A national blackjack coalition could preserve the game and maintain reasonable playing conditions by boycotting houses with unreasonable playing conditions.

A coalition could also bring about a genuine World Series of Blackjack, similar to the World Series of Poker, and encourage invitational tournaments in which the participants put up the prize money, with a percentage going to the house, the same way it is done in poker. It could also arrange overdue tribute dinners for such individuals as Edward O. Thorp and Julian H. Braun and be a source of enrichment for blackjack players throughout the country.

To be successful, we believe it would be necessary for the coalition to be nonprofit in structure and one in which no individual or group could benefit through marketing and promotion. Such an organization, with positive objectives and high ideals, could have an unprecedented impact on the gaming industry.

Recommended Reading

Blackjack marketing should be a constant concern of the New Era player. A number of industry-oriented publications are good sources to read about marketing trends, bankruptcies, and other relevant information.

The following publications are designed for executives and businesses that deal with the gaming industry:

Atlantic City Action, a newsletter focusing on New Jersey gaming, published monthly by Glasgow Associations, Inc., P.O. Box 5059, 33 S. Presbyterian Ave., Atlantic City, NJ 08404. The annual subscription rate is $100.

Casino Chronicle, a newsletter focusing on New Jersey gaming, published forty-eight times a year by Ben A. Borowsky, 2416 Laurel Drive, Cinnaminson, NJ 08077. The annual subscription rate is $135.

Gaming & Wagering Business, a magazine of the gaming industry published monthly by BMT Publications, Inc., Second Floor, 254 West 31st Street, New York, NY 10001. The annual subscription rate is $65.

Rouge et Noir News, a newsletter of casino gaming, published monthly by Rouge et Noir, Inc., P.O. Box 1146, Midlothian, VA 23223. The annual subscription rate is $50.

Glossary

Blackjack has a unique language. This glossary should give the novice player an understanding of the game of blackjack and also serve as a ready reference.

Bet. The amount of money wagered by a player against the dealer within betting limits established by the house. A table accepting $1 minimum bets may have a betting maximum of $300; a table with $5 minimum bets may have a betting maximum of $3,000. Signs are usually posted to inform players of betting minimums and maximums for each table.

Bias. Sometimes the result when randomness has been predictably inhibited, usually through the shuffling process. In general, a game in which the dealer is beating the majority of the players is considered a *dealer-biased* game; a game in which 50 percent or more of the players are defeating the dealer is considered a *player-biased* game.

Blackjack. A "natural," two-card "21" (a hand comprised of an ace and a 10-valued card) that is normally

169

paid a premium at three to two, unless the dealer also has a blackjack.

The word "Blackjack" has also replaced "21" as the name of a casino card game between a dealer and, usually, up to seven players. Cards are dealt in succession, with each player receiving two cards. The dealer also receives two cards, one of them exposed. The value of each hand is determined by adding the values of the two cards. Face cards count 10, and all other cards are worth their numerical value, except the ace, which counts as either 1 or 11, at the player's option.

The object of the game is to beat the dealer while not breaking (i.e., exceeding 21). Following the first deal of two cards, each player is allowed to draw additional cards or stand. If a player exceeds 21 or breaks, the bet is immediately lost. After each player has completed his or her turn, the dealer exposes the hole or unexposed card. If the dealer's hand totals 17 or more, no additional cards are drawn; if the hand totals 16 or less, the dealer must draw until achieving 17 or more. If the dealer exceeds 21, every player who has not exceeded 21 is automatically paid.

Break or Bust. A two-card total, by either the dealer or a player, exceeding 21. If a player breaks, he or she immediately loses the bet. If the dealer breaks, all players who did not bust automatically win their bets.

Burn Card. After the deck or decks are shuffled and cut, one card is placed at the bottom of the pack or in the discard tray. This is called burning a card. A few casinos burn more than one card, but this is not a common practice.

Chip or Check. A token used in lieu of money for betting. A $5 chip is worth $5. Chips are color-coded, and sometimes include the name or logo of the issuing house.

Counter. A player who uses a counting system to keep track of the types of cards played in order to determine whether the pack is mathematically favorable or unfavorable.

Cut. The process of splitting the deck or decks after the dealer has completed the shuffling process.

Cut Card. A solid-colored card, the same size as a playing card, used by a player to indicate a desired cut to the dealer. After the cut card is inserted into the deck or decks by the player, the cards are then cut at that location by the dealer.

Dealer. A casino employee who deals the game of blackjack, settles all bets, and supervises general play according to the house rules. The dealer plays his or her hand according to a predetermined set of rules, hitting all two-card totals of 16 or less.

Double Down. The doubling of a bet on the first two cards of a hand; in this case, the player will receive only one more card. For example, doubling down on 10 or 11 is advantageous because you are allowed to increase your bet after seeing the dealer's upcard; drawing a 10-valued card to that hand would give you a 20 or 21.

Flat bet. A bet of the same amount each time.

Game Control Methods. Procedures in which the house attempts to disrupt a game in which an excessive amount of money is being won by players. Such procedures may include simply changing the cards or introducing stripping, which, through rapid replications of single-card removal, reverses the order of the cards during the shuffling process. Another common method is the introduction of the unbalanced shuffle in which the dealer makes unequal picks for the purpose of inhibiting distribution. These game control methods do not represent forms of cheating and may not necessarily have an impact on the game.

Hard Hand. Any hand that totals 12 or more that does not include an ace, or any similar hand in which the ace is valued as 1. For example, a player drawing an ace to a two-card total of 16, would have a hard hand of 17.

Hit. The player's decision to take another card.

Hole Card. The unexposed card in the dealer's two-card hand; it is not shown until all of the players' hands have been played.

Insurance. A side bet when the dealer shows an ace upcard. The player is allowed to wager *up to half* of the original wager that the dealer's hole-card is a 10-valued card underneath, and thus a blackjack.

If the dealer does have blackjack, the insurance bet is paid off at two to one. The original bet, meanwhile, is lost, unless the player has a blackjack. If the player has a blackjack, the original bet is pushed. If the dealer does not have a blackjack, the player's insurance side bet is lost, and play continues.

Marker. A casino check or draft used by the player to draw chips against credit or money on deposit with the casino.

Pit Boss. A casino employee who supervises a number of blackjack dealers and floor personnel. "Pit boss" is sometimes inaccurately used to describe a floor person or general supervisor. Pit bosses are in charge of designated blackjack tables and consider requests for complimentary services from players, monitor inexperienced dealers, watch for cheating, referee floor disputes, and handle paperwork for scheduling employees. Floor personnel or general supervisors also monitor dealers and games while acting as hosts and hostesses to the players, particularly credit players.

Player's Advantage. The percentage of all money wagered that a player can expect to win in the long run. A player with a 2 percent advantage, therefore, can expect to win 2 percent of the total amount wagered.

Point Count. An evaluation of odds based on a numerical analysis of the pack. A number is assigned to each card according to the value of that card toward making up a winning hand for the player. In the high-low counting system, for example, each 2, 3, 4, 5, and 6 counts as plus one (+1); each 7, 8, or 9 counts as 0; each 10, J, Q, K, or ace counts as minus 1 (−1). The point count is computed at the end of each hand by totaling the value of each card played and combining the total with the value of all previous cards played. For example, if 6, 4, 10, ace, 8, and 3 were dealt off the top of a fresh deck, the point count would be plus one (+1). This is computed as follows: 6 (+1), 4 (+1), 10 (−1), ace (−1), 8 (0), and 3 (+1), totaling plus one (+1).

Push. A tie between the player and dealer; no money changes hands.

Rank. The defined value of each card. The 7 of hearts has a rank of 7. The king of clubs has a rank of 10.

Running Count. The point count updated as each card is played or dealt by the dealer instead of at the end of the round.

Shuffle-Tracking. A method of keeping track of specific cards through the shuffling procedure.

Soft Hand. Any hand containing an ace that totals 21 or less, with the ace valued as 11.

Split. A situation in which the player has two like cards, such as a pair of sevens. The player may play the cards as two separate hands, making another bet exactly equal to the original wager.

Stand. The player's decision not to take additional cards.

Stiff. Any hand between 12 and 16 in which the player or dealer has a chance of breaking.

Surrender. When the house rules permit, a decision made by a player to throw in the first two cards and surrender half the wager. If a player is allowed to make this play before the dealer turns over the hole card, it is called "early surrender." "Late surrender" enables a player to make the same play only after it has been determined that the dealer does not have a blackjack.

System or Strategy. The method of play. The basic strategy is an optimized method that involves rules for taking insurance, surrendering, splitting, doubling down, hitting, or standing. Other systems or strategies may involve card counting for determining the player's advantage or disadvantage and possible variation from basic strategy for the play of certain hands.

Table-Takeover. When as many as seven players take over all the spots at a blackjack table for the purpose of controlling the cut and predetermined shuffle-tracking objectives.

Toke. A tip or a wager placed for the dealer.

True Count. Running count adjusted to reflect the number of decks or cards remaining to be played. Also called the *count per deck*.

Selected Bibliography

Abram, Phil. "The Play of the General Public in Atlantic City Blackjack." Fifth National Conference on Gambling and Risk Taking, Stateline, NV, 1981.

Alvarez, A. *The Biggest Game in Town.* Boston: Houghton Mifflin Co., 1983.

Andersen, Ian. *Turning the Tables on Las Vegas.* New York: Vanguard, 1976.

Braun, Julian H. *How to Play Winning Blackjack.* Chicago: Data House Publishing Co., 1980.

Bristol, Claude M. *The Magic of Believing.* Englewood Cliffs, NJ: Prentice-Hall, Inc., 1948.

Canfield, Richard Albert. *Blackjack Your Way to Riches.* Scottsdale, AZ: Expertise Publishing Co., 1977.

Einstein, Charles. *How to Win at Blackjack.* Las Vegas: Gambler's Book Club Press, 1968.

Epstein, Richard A. *The Theory of Gambling and Statistical Logic.* New York: Academic Press, 1977.

Glass, Mary Ellen. *Nevada's Turbulent 50s.* Reno: University of Nevada Press, 1981.

Griffin, Peter A. *The Theory of Blackjack.* Las Vegas: Gambler's Book Club Press, 1979.

Humble, Lance. *Blackjack Gold.* Toronto: International Gaming, 1976. Retitled *Blackjack Super/Gold,* 1979.

Humble, Lance, and Carl Cooper. *The World's Greatest Blackjack Book.* Garden City, NY: Doubleday & Co., 1980.

Ita, Koko. *21 Counting Methods to Beat 21.* Las Vegas: Gambler's Book Club Press, 1976.

Karlins, Marvin. *Psyching Out Vegas.* Hollywood, CA: Gambling Times, Inc., 1983.

Mahon, Gigi. *The Company That Bought the Boardwalk.* New York: Random House, 1980.

Maltz, Maxwell. *Psycho-Cybernetics.* New York: Simon & Schuster, 1982.

Mandel, Leon. *William Fisk Harrah.* Garden City, NY: Doubleday & Co., 1982.

Ostrander, Sheila, and Lynn Schroeder. *Superlearning.* New York: Delta/The Confucian Press, 1979.

Patterson, Jerry L. *Blackjack: A Winner's Handbook.* Voorhees, NJ: Casino Gaming Specialists, 1977. Revised and expanded edition. New York: Perigee Books, 1982.

Patterson, Jerry L. *Blackjack's Winning Formula.* Voorhees, NJ: Casino Gaming Specialists, 1980. Revised and expanded edition. New York: Perigee Books, 1982.

Peter, Laurence J., and Bill Dana. *The Laughter Prescription.* New York: Ballantine Books, 1982.

Pritchard, Allyn, and Jean Taylor. *Accelerated Learning.* Novato, CA: Academic Therapy Publications, 1980.

Puzo, Mario. *Inside Las Vegas.* New York: Grosset & Dunlap, 1977.

Revere, Lawrence. *Playing Blackjack as a Business.* Secaucus, NJ: Lyle Stuart, 1977.

Roberts, Stanley. *The Gambling Times Guide to Blackjack.* Hollywood, CA: Gambling Times, Inc., 1984.

Roberts, Stanley. *Winning Blackjack.* Los Angeles: Scientific Research Services, 1973.

Selye, Hans. *Stress Without Distress.* New York: Harper & Row, 1974.

Smith, Raymond. *The Poker Kings of Las Vegas.* Dublin: Aherlow Publishers, Ltd., 1982.

Snyder, Arnold. *The Blackjack Formula*. Berkeley, CA: R. G. Enterprises, 1980.

Snyder, Arnold. *Blackjack for Profit*. Berkeley, CA: R. G. Enterprises, 1981.

Sternlieb, George, and James W. Hughes. *The Atlantic City Gamble*. Cambridge, MA: Harvard University Press, 1983.

Stone, W. Clement. *The Success System That Never Fails*. New York: Simon & Schuster, 1983.

Thorp, Edward O. *Beat the Dealer*. New York: Random House, 1962. Revised version. New York: Vintage Books, 1966.

Uston, Ken. *Million Dollar Blackjack*. Los Angeles: SRS Enterprises, 1981.

Uston, Ken. *Two Books on Blackjack*. Wheaton, MD: Uston Institute of Blackjack, 1979.

Uston, Ken, and Roger Rapoport. *The Big Player*. New York: Holt, Rinehart and Winston, 1977.

Waitley, Denis. *The Psychology of Winning*. Chicago: Nightingale-Conant Corp., 1979; New York: Berkley Books, 1984.

Waitley, Denis. *Seeds of Greatness*. Old Tappan, NJ: Fleming H. Revell Co., 1983.

Wilson, Allan N. *The Casino Gambler's Guide*. Enlarged Edition. New York: Harper & Row, 1977.

Wong, Stanford. "Counter–Casino Confrontation Symposium." Fifth National Conference on Gambling and Risk Taking, Stateline, NV, 1981.

Wong, Stanford. *Professional Blackjack*. Las Vegas: Gambler's Book Club Press, 1977. Revised version. La Jolla, CA: Pi Yee Press, 1980.

Ziglar, Zig. *See You at the Top*. Gretna, LA: Pelican Publishing Co., 1974.

About the Authors

Jerry Patterson has developed a national reputation as a provider of consumer-oriented gaming information. His three casino gaming books—*Blackjack: A Winner's Handbook, Blackjack's Winning Formula,* and *Casino Gambling*—have been acclaimed as the best in the field for both novice and experienced players alike. His book *Sports Betting: A Winner's Handbook* is the most comprehensive in the field of sports handicapping yet published.

Jerry Patterson owns and operates, with his wife, Nancy, a very successful blackjack school with more than ten thousand graduates. His syndicated casino gaming columns have been published by such prestigious newspapers as the Philadelphia *Inquirer,* the New York *Daily News,* the San Francisco *Chronicle,* and the Los Angeles *Herald Examiner.*

Prior to becoming a professional gambler in 1980, he was vice-president and cofounder of Systems & Computer Technology Corp., a national computer-services company.

Jerry holds a Bachelor of Science degree in mathematics from Willamette University (1956) and a Master of Science degree in computer science from George Washington University (1968).

Jerry played his first hand of casino blackjack in 1956 and holds the distinction of being the codeveloper of the first computerized blackjack model in the early 1960s.

Eddie Olsen, one of blackjack's most successful players, is the innovator of numerous shuffle-tracking techniques and is the inventor of TARGET, a table-selection and departure method. He is also the first known player to develop a method for tracking the single-deck game, cutting favorable cards into play or unfavorable cards out of play.

Olsen has averaged 2,500 hours a year inside Nevada and New Jersey casinos, but says he tries not to take himself or his blackjack activities too seriously. "Blackjack is just a card game," he says. "For me, it's a lot of hard work."

Nicknamed "The Chocolate Kid" because of his preference for the color brown, Olsen is currently working on two additional books and lives with his wife, Rita, in Hilltown, Pa. He has an extensive journalism background, working for newspapers in Oregon, California, and Indiana, and is presently a columnist with the Philadelphia *Inquirer.* He has three sons, Mark, John, and Steven.

Appendix A   Blackjack Products and Services Offered by Jerry Patterson

1. Other Blackjack Books by Jerry L. Patterson

Use the coupon on the last page to request ordering data for these books if you can't find them at your local bookstore.

Blackjack: A Winner's Handbook

This book contains a review of the entire blackjack field including blackjack books, card-counting systems, newsletters and magazines, and instructional programs. Written in 1977 and revised and expanded in 1982, this book is still a must for the serious player's library. A plan for player development is included which offers beginning, intermediate, and advanced programs. The book includes a complete and comprehensive bibliography.

Blackjack's Winning Formula

This book is a primer for the student who desires to beat the game. It explains the rudiments of the game for the novice player. The book includes basic strategy, card-counting, and money management techniques for both Atlantic City and Nevada. Some of Jerry's blackjack adventures in Nevada, Atlantic

City, and the Caribbean are highlighted. Excellent chapters are included that point up the advantages of the female blackjack player.

Casino Gambling

This book is a primer on all casino table games: blackjack, craps, roulette, and baccarat. The rules of play are explained and winning strategies are presented. A special chapter is included on tournament blackjack.

2. The TARGET Instructional Program— Course Outline

The TARGET Method was described in Chapter 9. It is offered as both a Home Study Package or a Weekend Class Experience in Atlantic City, Las Vegas, or Reno/Tahoe. The course outline below includes, in addition, a Basic Strategy and Card-Counting Course.

LESSON 1: UNDERSTANDING TARGET AND WHY YOU WIN
   (Audio Tapes)
   TARGET Factors: How to Select a Money-Making Table
   How One TARGET Superfactor Can Almost Guarantee
      Your Profits
   When to Leave the Table with Profits in Hand
   How and Why TARGET Solves the Problems Associated
      with Card-Counting
   How to use TARGET to Pick Tables Where the Count
      Really Works
   Definitions of Bias and Nonrandom Shuffles and How They
      Work to Your Advantage
   Why the "Wash" Makes Certain Games Off-Limits
   Understanding the Different Types of Shuffles and How
      They Work to Your Advantage or Disadvantage
   Special Drills for TARGET Casino Practice

LESSON 2: EXPLOITING TARGET'S PROFIT POTENTIAL

Questions and Answers from a Live TARGET Classroom Session

How to Increase Your Profits by Using a Disciplined Documentation Method

Money Management: Flat Betting (the Same Amount) and When to Use It

Money Management: When to Bet and When Not to Bet with the Count

Money Management: Special Techniques for Recreational Gamblers, High Rollers, and Junket Players

Tips for Creating the "Home Run Tables" Where the Dealer Breaks Hand After Hand

How to "Tune" Your Play to Exploit the Special Advantages in the Atlantic City Game

Nuances for the Variety of Games in Nevada

"Action TARGET": Amazing Money-Making Opportunities for Nevada's Single-Deck Games

When and How to Avoid Losing by Standing on Stiff Hands

How to Evaluate a Casino for TARGET play

LESSON 3: TARGET CASINO SESSION (Two hours in the casino with Jerry and a small group)

How the Casino Session Works

Instructor Selects TARGET Tables for Review and Comment

Students Practice Scouting and Table Selection with Instructor Feedback

Instructor Monitors Table Departure

TARGET COURSE MATERIALS

Six hours of Audiocassette tape on TARGET

Two Hours of Video Tape: Basic Strategy, Card-Counting, and TARGET

TARGET Manual

A Portfolio of Expanded TARGET Course Materials
Basic Strategy Course Materials
Card-Counting Course Materials
Casino Evaluation Report
Access to Blackjack Hotline
Follow-up: Consultation, Conferences, and Conventions

Appendix B   Blackjack Products and Services Offered by Eddie Olsen

One of today's most innovative blackjack strategists, Eddie Olsen does not offer personal consultation. He does, however, publish ten times a year a newsletter called *Blackjack Confidential,* which monitors and recommends blackjack games throughout the world. The newsletter has a number of blackjack features to sharpen skills and strategies, and also stresses ways to save time, energy, and money. Coverage includes human development advancements, blackjack marketing strategies, and general industry news and trends. The price for a one-year subscription (ten issues) is $95. (See p. 186 for subscription order form.)

--------- SUBSCRIPTION ORDER FORM ---------

BLACKJACK CONFIDENTIAL
21 Pineside Drive
Perkasie, PA 18944

Enclosed is $95. Please send me one year (10 issues) of Eddie Olsen's *Blackjack Confidential*.

Name _____

Street Address _____

City _____

Telephone _____

Appendix C   Other Gambling Products and Services Offered by Jerry Patterson

New Power/Pace Handicapping Method

*An Amazing Breakthrough in Thoroughbred and
Standardbred Handicapping*
REALIZE A 50 PERCENT OR BETTER RETURN ON YOUR INVESTMENT!

*For Just an Hour Per Racing Day
And So Simple You Can Even Handicap Between Races at the Track*

I have been doing extensive research for the last two years on winning methods for horse-race handicapping. That research has recently culminated in a totally new and winning method called Power/Pace. Power/Pace is a very powerful money-making tool and I invite you to inquire about how to become a Power/Pace user. The key features of Power/Pace are outlined below. Use the coupon to request more details on home study learning packages or weekend class experiences.

Time: You can handicap an entire nine-race card in less than an hour. You can handicap between races while at the track.

Return-on-Investment: Our research has shown that you will earn 50 percent or more on each dollar wagered. The average price per winning horse is well above $8.

Simplicity: There is nothing complicated about the method. The most difficult part is dividing one number by another, as 8 ÷ 4 = 2.

Action: You will play five to eight races per card.

Coverage: You can easily play more than one track if you are in a position to do so as with New York OTB or the Las Vegas Race Books.

Location: You do not have to be at the track to bet your selections. You can use "early bird" betting, phone betting, or go to the track, make your bets, and return home before the races are run.

Exotic Bets: The method works very well with exactas, trifectas and quinielas. You can even use it to play the "Pick 6" and go for the super payoffs.

Streaks: Long losing streaks rarely occur if at all. Very seldom will you lose three races in a row. On the other hand, long winning streaks are quite common because you are winning over 60 percent of the races played (assuming you're betting two horses per race to win).

Short Learning Curve: In a matter of a few hours or a few days, you will have mastered the Power/Pace method.

Sports Betting

You can win at sports betting. Not just for one game or a season. But consistently and permanently. Season after season. Find out how by reading Jerry's book: *Sports Betting: A Winner's Handbook.* Coauthored with the book is a complete guide to sports handicapping systems and methods for football, basketball, and baseball betting.

Use the coupon to request information on sports seminars, home study courses, and to purchase a copy of the book if you can't find it at your local bookstore.

Players Club International

There is an important new development in the gambling field that I would like to share with you—the formation of Players Club International. The Club has been organized to bring all of the casino benefits—heretofore only available to high rollers and players with large credit lines—to occasional and recreational gamblers and weekend players.

When you start your membership, tell Players Club that you found out about it though me or my book, and you will get a very special bonus worth more than the membership cost of $100. Call or write to us, and we will send you this special offer in a brochure.

Here's what you receive for the membership:

Guaranteed Savings: A minimum of 25 percent to 60 percent off your hotel room rate. Off meals and drinks: 25 percent, even at the gourmet restaurants in member casinos. Twenty-five percent off shows for up to four people.

VIP Privileges: Pass by the show lines for immediate VIP entrance, special check-in area that avoids lines, invitations to casino parties and sporting events.

Monthly Hot Sheet: Features special room rates and prices at various casinos, contests, and other good deals.

Hotel Reservations: One call to Players Club and they will get you into your hotel at the special rates.

Car Rentals: Discounts at major car-rental agencies.

Accommodations are at first class casino/hotels in Nevada, Atlantic City, and other international locations.

Call us *today* to receive your brochure: 1 (800) 257-7130

Information Request Form

Please send this form or a copy to:

Jerry Patterson's Blackjack Clinic
Box 777
1133 Thackary Court
Voorhees, New Jersey 08043

For faster service call toll free: 1 (800) 257-7130
In New Jersey call: 1 (609) 772-2721

- -

☐ Blackjack TARGET Method. Please send me a FREE 12-page brochure on this winning method.

☐ Please call me at the telephone number below and tell me about a simple demonstration of a blackjack table bias that will show me how your TARGET program works.

☐ Power/Pace Handicapping Method for Thoroughbred and Standardbred Horse Racing. Please send me a brochure on this winning method.

☐ Sports Betting. Please send information on your Sports Investors Network.

☐ Players Club International. Please send information package with your special offer.

☐ I would like to purchase copies of Jerry's books. Please send a list of prices.
  ☐ *Blackjack: A Winner's Handbook*
  ☐ *Blackjack's Winning Formula*
  ☐ *Casino Gambling*
  ☐ *Sports Betting: A Winner's Handbook*

☐ Stock Option Power Move Strategy. I would like to find out more about how to make money by trading stock options.

☐ Please send information on:
  ☐ TARGET Home Study Course and Casino Session
  ☐ TARGET Weekend Classes with Jerry Patterson
  ☐ Card Counting Instruction

- -

Name _____

Street Address _____

City _____

Telephone _____